Leaders
With
Vision

CORWIN
PRESS

The Corwin Press logo—a raven striding across an open book—represents the happy union of courage and learning. We are a professional-level publisher of books and journals for K-12 educators, and we are committed to creating and providing resources that embody these qualities. Corwin's motto is "Success for All Learners."

Leaders With Vision

The Quest for School Renewal

Robert J. Starratt

CORWIN PRESS, INC.
A Sage Publications Company
Thousand Oaks, California

For information address:

Corwin Press, Inc.
A Sage Publications Company
2455 Teller Road
Thousand Oaks, California 91320
E-mail: order@corwin.sagepub.com

SAGE Publications Ltd.
6 Bonhill Street
London EC2A 4PU
United Kingdom

SAGE Publications India Pvt. Ltd.
M-32 Market
Greater Kailash I
New Delhi 110 048 India

Printed in the United States of America

Library of Congress Cataloging-in-Publication Data

Starratt, Robert J.
　　Leaders with vision: The quest for school renewal / Robert J.
Starratt
　　　　p. cm.
　　Reworking of: Transforming life in schools.
　　Includes bibliographical references and index.
　　ISBN 0-8039-6259-2 (cloth: alk. paper). — ISBN 0-8039-6260-6
(pbk.: alk. paper)
　　　　1. Educational leadership—United States.　2. School management
and organization—United States.　3. School administrators—United
States.　4. Teacher participation in administration—United States.
5. Educational change—United States.　I. Starratt, Robert J.
Transforming life in schools.　II. Title.
LB805.S744　1995
371.2'00973—dc20　　　　　　　　　　　　　　　　　　　95-22650

This book is printed on acid-free paper.

95　96　97　98　99　10　9　8　7　6　5　4　3　2　1

Corwin Press Production Editor: Gillian Dickens　　Typesetter: Christina Hill

Contents

Preface   ix

About the Author   xiii

1. The Principal as Leader of School Reform   1

   Turbulence in Education Reflected
     in the Wider Society   3
   The Principal as Agent of
     Multiple Constituencies   5
   Working Smarter   7
   The Principal as Educational Leader   8
   Summing Up   10

2. A New Vision and Theory of Leadership   13

   A Theory of Leadership With Vision   14
   Expressing a Vision   15
   Sources of Vision   16
   Vision and Reflective Practice   19
   Summing Up   21

3. **Leadership and the Sense of Drama**   **23**

    Forming a Character for the Drama   23
    Forming a People   26
    Forming Civil Society   26
    Living the Drama of History   29
    Hope From the Scientific Community   31
    The Multiple Roles of the Principal   32
    Summing Up   34

4. **The Empowering Covenant**   **37**

    What Is Power?   39
    Empowerment as Personal and
      Professional Fulfillment   41
    Empowerment of a Community   44
    Empowering Ideas and Ideals   44
    Organizing for Empowerment   45
    Summing Up   46

5. **Leadership and Institutional Transformation**   **47**

    The Paradox of Institutional Life   48
    A Model for Schools as Institutions   50
    Teaming Up Leadership With Administration   55
    Summing Up   58

6. **Leadership and Reflective Practice**   **61**

    Ongoing Renewal of the Vision   62
    The Reflective Practitioner   63
    Reflective Practice   66
    Summing Up   76

7. **Education as Personal Formation:**
    Plots, Players, and Possibilities   **77**

    The Plots   79
    The Players   88
    The Possibilities   93
    Summing Up   94

8. **The Politics of Reform and the Life World**   **95**

    The Life World   96
    The World of Mass Administration
       and Production   96
    Colonization of the Life World   97
    Separation of the Life World of Children
       From That of Adults   99
    Imagining Other Possibilities   100
    Summing Up   103

9. **The Moral Leadership of School Reform**   **105**

    Moral Leadership   106
    Leadership of the Principal   108
    Transactional and Transformational Leadership   109
    Leadership and the State   113
    A Paradigm Shift   117
    Summing Up   118

    References   119

    Index   123

Preface

One would think by now we've read enough on leadership, and certainly, on school renewal. It seems that books have been gushing forth in recent years on educational leadership, transformational leadership, the instructional leadership of the principal, empowering leadership, moral leadership, leadership and school transformation, restructuring schools, and renewing schools. What more could possibly be said on the topic? Quite simply, what I offer in this book is a theory of leadership and an exploration of the larger intellectual landscape of leadership that poses challenges to educators well beyond what passes for renewal in the literature.

This is not to say that others haven't been saying what will be found between these covers. I offer an integrated synthesis of the elements developed by others that constitute the essence of educational leadership. I provide, then, a distinct and unique focus for principals and teachers. This synthesis takes up Chapters 2 through 6. In the final three chapters, I explore some foundational meanings that should be part of, or stand behind, the vision of educating leaders for tomorrow's schools.

This book has grown out of 20 years of studying and teaching leadership to educators. That work included designing a variety of graduate programs for educators who aspired to leadership in the schools. That work also involved designing and conducting intensive residential workshops of several weeks' duration with educators in the United States and elsewhere, especially in Pacific Rim countries, and most especially in Australia. A few years ago, some colleagues in Australia asked me to put together a collection of papers I had given on the topic Leadership and School Renewal. The result was a publication by the Australian Council on Educational Administration (ACEA) called *Transforming Life in Schools: Conversations About Leadership and School Renewal.* That book was favorably received in Australia, and through a limited distribution, in the United States. Conversations with Gracia Alkema of Corwin Press led me to believe that a reworking of that text with a sharper focus on school renewal in this country would find a welcome reception in the United States. The ACEA graciously granted permission to rework the original text for a U.S. audience.

This book is written for principals and teachers who wish to exercise leadership in the ongoing work of school renewal. But I do not address the book solely to administrators, as the work of renewal requires the collaborative leadership of both teachers and administrators. The theory of leadership I develop in this book supports leadership work of teachers and administrators alike. I attempt to show the organic link between a vision of education and the institutionalization of changes that reflect that vision. I also offer ideas and ideals that might make up such a vision of schooling.

For educators whose horizon rarely rises above daily school crises, this book may appear hopelessly idealistic. Although I would argue with the adverb *hopelessly,* I wear the name tag of idealist proudly. I believe that educators need to look beyond the managing of messes (although messes will, like the bills, always be there) to the possibilities of the human spirit. There is so much potential in young people. There are such wonderful and amazing things to learn. There are so many beautiful things human beings can make together. There are such momentous challenges our society is facing. There is a new world order waiting to be realized. Schools can be exciting, challenging, fulfilling places if the people in them believe in themselves enough to make them that way. In this book, I attempt to nurture the hopeful perspective that can fuel the work of renewal.

Beyond hopefulness, I offer a deeper look at what "the vision thing" means and how others can be invited to compose a communal vision that bonds and energizes the community. Perhaps the strongest part of the leadership theory is the insistence that leaders recreate the institution so that it embodies the vision in its structures and processes. This entails a closer analysis of the policies, programs, and organizational arrangements that often impede the vision, and that when reconfigured, can carry the vision into the routines of everyday school life. Beyond this first achievement of institutionalizing the vision, leadership is called upon to continually refresh the vision and the institution by close attention to the regular rituals and ceremonies of the school and by communal practice of reflection within the workday. Another focus within this leadership framework is attention to students and to their leadership possibilities within the school community. In short, this approach to leadership is intended to develop leadership throughout the learning community.

Finally, educators need to look at the larger context in which schools are situated. Schools are affected by the larger political, economic, social, and cultural forces in society. We have heard of the need for educational leaders to become much more sensitive to the multicultural communities schools are called upon to serve. Likewise, leaders must align the school with the needs of the 21st-century workforce. Beyond that, they are urged to keep in mind the global realities as well as the environmental challenges of the 21st century. One challenge seldom is mentioned—namely, the challenge to the human life world itself. In Chapter 8, I encourage educators to be aware of that challenge. There is the challenge, also, of educating for mature citizenship. In Chapter 9, I look at how that challenge speaks to the moral leadership of the principal.

I would like to acknowledge the long-standing support of Brian Caldwell of the University of Melbourne. For at least a decade Brian has been dragging me all around Australia telling me that I had something important to say. He also supported the publication of the progenitor of this book during his presidency of ACEA. I also want to thank his colleague at Melbourne, Dr. Hedley Beare, who wrote some kind words about the ACEA book. Beside their support, I treasure

their friendship. I must also thank my wife, Ruth, for her encourage-
ment, support, and patience. Beside reading much of the manuscript,
she has surrendered me with good grace to many summer days and
occasional long night hours with the word processor—time in which
I rightfully belonged to her. She has the small consolation of knowing
that whatever of the best part of me is in this book, she shares in that.

ROBERT J. STARRATT

About the Author

Robert J. Starratt is Professor and Chair, Division of Administration, Policy and Urban Education, in the Graduate School of Education of Fordham University in New York City. His scholarly interests include the areas of leadership, curriculum, and human resource development. Recent books include *The Drama of Schooling/The Schooling of Drama* (1990), *The Drama of Leadership* (1993), *Building an Ethical School* (1994), and *Supervision: A Redefinition* (with Thomas J. Sergiovanni, 1993).

⋐ 1 ⋑

The Principal as
Leader of School Reform

In the United States, we have been going through a decade or more of intensive efforts at school reform and renewal. This effort began in a top-down fashion, with the federal and then the state governments, strongly influenced by the business community, pointing to the low achievement of U.S. students compared to European and Asian students and demanding a more rigorous curriculum to restore U.S. competitiveness among the community of nations. State governors and legislators proposed longer school years, longer school days, and more years of required "meat-and-potatoes" subjects such as math and science and foreign languages. These initiatives seemed to equate more with better. Critics have pointed out that it does not improve a failing system to increase the amounts of the very treatments that have been failing. They proposed that the whole system of schooling needed rethinking and restructuring.

A second wave of school reform initiatives was led by the teaching profession and university schools of education. This was a more bottom-up approach to renewal. The reformers proposed increased attention to teachers' professional development, both in initial preparation programs and in ongoing professional training. Coupled with site-based management, these measures were to enable and empower teachers to redesign the school and its curriculum so as to improve student achievement. In this second wave of reform, more attention was to be given to the *context* in which teaching and learning took place. Greater sensitivity to multicultural issues in schools serving multicultural communities, new approaches to education of handicapped or challenged children, new involvements of schools with local industries and universities, new forms of parental involvement, new possibilities for learning in community settings—these and other local initiatives would be called for. Local school-based committees of teachers would work out internal redesign of programs; school-based committees of teachers and parents would decide on the major policy guidelines. All of this, of course, was to take place within overall policies set by the state and federal educational agencies. The agenda of schooling within these initiatives, however, still appeared to be dominated almost exclusively by a concern to promote a better-educated workforce to support the U.S. economy.

This second wave of reform itself generated what some call a third wave of reform, concerned with the leadership of schools. This wave centers on three major issues. The first concerns the management of the difficult transition from traditional-style schools to schools for the 21st century. Due to the enormous complexity of this transition, a different kind of administrator is called for than the one traditionally concerned with bureaucratic demands of managing the status quo (if there ever was a status quo that lasted for more than a week!). This new challenge calls for leadership, but a leadership different from that typically described in the previous round of literature on leadership. The new leadership will have to be much more involved in supporting the work of the professional staff, creating and working within networks, and nurturing organic organizational patterns rather than hierarchical organizational patterns of authority.

The second issue deals with the purposes of schooling. These new educational leaders will have to be much more involved with shaping schools that are responsive to the emerging needs of the

community and of the larger society, not only in regard to the changing context of the world of work and employment, but also with
reference to the political, cultural, and social changes taking place. In
the process of redesigning schools, these new leaders will have to
integrate organizational engineering with social engineering. The
new leaders will have to attune themselves to social policy developments within both the private and state sectors and participate in the
shaping of the policies. This calls for a new kind of intellectual and
political leadership among principals. As Foster (1989) said, the new
leaders will have to be transformative intellectuals (though they
should keep the use of such fancy language to themselves). Educators need to think of themselves as part of the policy discussion, not
simply implementers of policy someone else decides on, and the discussion has to go beyond arguments for job security and decent
wages to a concern for what the schools should be teaching and in
what variety of formats.

The third issue is the preparation and selection of these new leaders. What will be the standards and criteria for selection and preparation and ongoing education of such leaders? Assisted by multiyear
support from the Danforth Foundation, networks of major universities in the United States with degree programs in educational administration have begun a serious conversation about overhauling their
curricula and degree requirements, with a view to preparing administrators to meet the two leadership challenges I have just referred to.

Turbulence in Education
Reflected in the Wider Society

The turbulence in the educational world is reflected, of course,
in the turbulence of the wider society. The U.S. economy is currently
undergoing major stress in adjusting to a new world order and to the
transformation from labor-intensive to knowledge-intensive work.
Peter Drucker has called our attention to this transformation in his
incisive book *The New Realities* (1989). As institutional effectiveness
and productivity become increasingly dependent on knowledge-
intensive technologies, old jobs are being phased out, other jobs are

being upgraded, and new but fluid jobs are emerging. Drucker (1989) refers to the new worldview necessitated by the new global order, paradoxical limits and new functions of government, and "postbusiness society," which has been superseded by the knowledge society. In the knowledge society, knowledge is the economy's foundation and its true capital. Access to and the development of knowledge, rather than the amassing of huge profits, is what will guarantee any institution a future.

Moreover, as Jeffrey Lustig (1987), a scholar of economic history advocates, ownership and decision-making power must be shared more equitably in those corporations that depend on the intelligence and initiative of all their members, not simply the entrepreneurs. Along with other economists and political scientists, Bellah and his associates, in their recent book *The Good Society* (Bellah, Madsen, Sullivan, Swidler, & Tipton, 1991), contend that the whole economic system in the United States requires a new sense of direction toward global and national responsibility—a sense of economic citizenship in which the whole economy becomes more democratic. This of course would mean an enormous shift in attitudes in the United States about the so-called pure market economy, which theoretically should never suffer the taint of government regulation. But the myth of the individual economic actor acting out of self-interest as the sole foundation of the U.S. economy is being seen as more and more dysfunctional. This economy pollutes the environment, impoverishes our inner cities, places heavy anxieties about job security on most workers, and attempts to reduce every aspect of life to cost-benefit analysis. Without public consensus on a common good that economic decisions must honor and seek, the U.S. economy will self-destruct.

These new realities create a state of continuous turbulence for those who would manage institutions—what Peter Vaill (1989) refers to as the state of perpetual white water. Administrators used to handle periodic crises with the understanding that things would soon settle back to normal—the normality of, for example, campers in a canoe paddling from one river to another. In the transition from the calm waters of one river to the next, one must pass through rapids, but that is a temporary moment of high adventure before reaching the next river. Vaill (1989) observes that the rapidly changing social, technological, economic, and political environment makes it impossible for managers to develop long-term plans, stay with fixed organizational patterns, and measure institutional effectiveness by the familiar standards. It is becoming impossible for managers to ever know enough to stay on top of their jobs. Longer days at the office, weekend reading about new developments in their field, attending seminars and workshops on new technologies—these used to keep managers prepared to lead their institution safely into the future. Not anymore. The rules of the game now are constantly changing, and this situation shows no signs of going away. The leaders of tomorrow's institutions will have to live with the tensions, contradictions, ambiguities, and unpredictability of perpetual turbulence.

One of the causes of turbulence is the dynamic social context of institutions themselves. Institutions are accountable to a variety of stakeholders—customers or clients, stockholders, state regulatory agencies, political interest groups, labor unions, professional organizations, and so on. These in turn are influenced by larger trends and upheavals in the broader society. From this perspective, I want to speak first of the school principal as an agent of many communities and constituencies. Then I would like to speak of what I perceive to be the leadership required of principals in guiding schools during these turbulent times.

The Principal as
Agent of Multiple Constituencies

The principal is an agent of multiple constituencies. One of these constituencies is the state. It is the principal's responsibility to carry out the policies and directives of the state in furthering the best education possible for the children in a given school. Yet the principal is not a mindless robot, but rather a member of a community of educators. That community should have some part in the policy discussions before the policies are enacted by the state. Principals need to keep abreast of policy initiatives being considered by the state. Through local and state associations of educators, principals can have a voice in these policy deliberations. The principal is also the agent of the local community, serving the parents who send their children to that school and attempting to nurture an educational environment that is responsive to the needs of their children. Parents have a right to complain if their children are being adversely affected by school experiences. Principals and teachers have to work as a team with families to respond to the needs of the children.

The principal must also answer to another constituency, the educational profession. It is the principal's responsibility to promote the best professional practice in the school, to confront shoddy or inappropriate practices in the classroom and on the school grounds by the professional staff, to celebrate outstanding work of both students and staff, and to provide professional development opportunities for the staff. It is the principal's responsibility to keep the school community focused on the essential function of the school, namely high-quality teaching and high-quality learning. Finally, the principal has to be an advocate for children. The principal is the one who often must interpret the proper course of action for particular children who do not fit the standard operating procedures or who are at risk of failing because of bad home situations.

It is seldom easy to balance the responsibilities to all these constituencies, especially when two or more of them appear to be in conflict. But it is important during this time of turbulence for principals to remember they always had the responsibility to interpret policy to fit individual circumstances. Principals do neither the state nor the profession a service when they apply policy uniformly to all situations, as though every child, every teacher, every classroom, and every teachable moment were the same. With reference to "taking the heat in the kitchen," I believe this is where the job of the principal is the hottest, because policies are shifting, accountability is shifting, and the rules seem to be changing all the time. It is hotter in the kitchen, to be sure, but the responsibility to make discretionary decisions that in the judgment of the principal will benefit this child, this teacher, this family in these circumstances has always been part of the job. There is no guarantee that every decision will be the best or the right one; no mechanism yet devised can guarantee that. In turbulent times, one always has to keep the purpose of the enterprise in mind—in this case, the best learning for all of the children in a given school.

But that raises the question, "What *is* the best learning?" To respond to that question, I will refer to three major purposes of schooling, namely, the intellectual, the moral, and the social purposes. Although separate, in practice these interpenetrate and complement one another. The intellectual purpose means learning the truth—the truth about ourselves, the truth about our human heritage, the truth about our local community, the truth about our national history, the truth about the natural world we live in. The moral purpose means learning autonomy, creativity, community, freedom, responsibility, and the discipline to exercise those virtues. The social purpose means preparing youngsters for the world of work and the world of citizenship. We hear much these days about preparing youngsters with basic learning in language, science, and math for the world of work, but we do not hear enough about preparing them for involvement in public life. Youngsters need to be encouraged to vote, to be sure, but they also need to learn how public policy is formulated and how the various institutions operate through which they can participate in debate about the common good. Joseph Featherstone (1988) captures these three purposes of education:

> We educate students to make meanings and lives, as well as livings. Making a living is a pressing, even desperate concern for many of our students, and rightly so in uncertain times; but they also need to learn how to make a life, and, beyond that, to take part in a democratic culture that doesn't yet exist. (p. 5)

All three purposes of schooling must be honored equally. They are so intertwined that to ignore one will necessarily weaken the other two. Principals who keep those purposes clearly in mind will be able to make the prudent judgments they have to make in implementing state and local policies.

Working Smarter

Peter Vaill (1989) offers suggestions for managers in the business field as they try to cope with the state of perpetual turbulence. He suggests that managers need to work smarter, not harder (they are already working too hard). But working smarter in a world of continually changing rules is difficult. Working smarter means working *collectively* smarter, that is, working with the collective intelligence of everyone in the organization. Working smarter also means working *reflectively* smarter, that is, taking the time, in the midst of rapid change, to gain perspective, to see the larger picture, to assess the pros and cons of the suggested changes, and to anticipate the unanticipated consequences. Working smarter also means working *spiritually* smarter, says Vaill (1989), referring to staying in touch with your own human spirit and with the humanity of those around you, letting your actions be guided by your best intuitions of what the deepest aspirations of humans tell you about the directions and decisions you should take. Of course, this task requires ongoing attempts to center on the deep human values and aspirations you read in yourself and in other spokespersons of the human spirit.

Vaill's (1989) suggestions imply that principals have to consult their staff continually, not only on day-to-day problems, but also on the big policy questions and challenges. They must take time to review the various national and state directives fluttering down like a continuous snowfall from the sky, time to see whether these directives can support local efforts at quality education, or whether they will, albeit unintentionally, thwart local efforts at quality education. Principals will have to spend more time probing their deepest convictions about the education of children and youth, and about the central human values involved in that education. They may find a new way to conduct teaching and learning in the school itself: collectively, reflectively, and spiritually. If we are preparing the next generation for involvement in a world of permanent change, perhaps we should start building up those habits early on.

The Principal as Educational Leader

At this point, I want to address the principal's leadership. I start with a quick diversion through the field of leadership studies. After gaining perspective from this overview, we may be able to interpret more clearly the job of the principal during these turbulent times.

Major shifts in theory and research on leadership have taken place in the last 15 years or so. I won't go on about the details of this shift or recite the various scholars involved. Looking over the highlights, one might say that there has been a major shift from a focus on *functional* leadership to a focus on *substantive* leadership—that is, from leadership fueled by functional rationality to leadership fueled by substantive rationality. *Functional rationality* is a way of thinking that focuses on means rather than on ends, on efficiency and technical problem solving, rather than on the significance of the final product. *Substantive rationality* implies keeping the larger purposes of the organization in mind and letting those closest to the various tasks of the organization figure out the everyday details. Substantive rationality is a way of thinking that involves asking, "Why are we doing this?" "What does it mean?" "What is its value to society, to human life?"

Leaders energized by substantive purpose and significance communicate that sense of purpose and significance to their colleagues. People throughout the organization have a greater sense of what they are collectively achieving, what value they are bringing to the world. And that sense of value and significance brings a sense of fulfillment to their working lives.

With this shift to a focus on substantive leadership, there has developed a tendency to distinguish leadership from administration or management.[1] Sometimes that distinction can take on dichotomized qualities that seem opposed to each other (see Table 1.1).

The polarized categories seen in Table 1.1 are self-explanatory. Obviously, such polarizations, although serving the purpose of highlighting differences in pure forms of leadership and administration, do not conform to reality. In most cases, leaders have to manage, and if they can't, they had better hire a good administrator and work closely with that person. A more realistic view is of the leader-manager, or a leader-manager team, such as illustrated in Table 1.2.

School-based leadership will always be exercised in the zone between demands and constraints (Fullan, 1991; Sergiovanni, 1990; Starratt, 1993). Expectations and demands that are not fulfilled can lead to the loss of one's job. Union agreements may constrain certain collaborative efforts between parents and teachers. However, within the demands and constraints, there are many possibilities for leadership. There are many measures principals and teachers can take that are neither required nor prohibited. Although the opportunities for leadership are not limitless, principals can initiate alternatives to

Table 1.1 Polarized Qualities of Leaders and Administrators

Leader	Administrator
Is concerned with growth	Is concerned with maintenance
Is a director	Is a stage manager
Writes the script	Follows the script
Based in moral authority	Based in loyalty and bureaucratic authority
Challenges people	Keeps people happy
Has vision	Has lists, schedules, budgets
Exercises power of shared purpose	Exercises power of sanctions and rewards
Defines what is real as what is possible	Defines what is real as what is
Motivates	Controls
Inspires	Fixes
Illuminates	Coordinates

routine practice in many ways. One way of exercising leadership in a time of many directives from the federal and state authorities is to study the meaning behind them, searching for justifiable interpretations that are consistent with a desired course of action.

Summing Up

It is clear that the calls for reform and renewal of the schools require a response of leadership. I have tried to indicate that the kind of leadership required is more than technical proficiency and functional rationality. Although those are needed, what is needed even more is a leadership of substance—a leadership of ideas, of vision, of

Table 1.2 Collaboration of Leadership and Managerial Talent

Leader	Leader-Manager Team	Manager
Is concerned with growth	Is concerned with institutional growth	Is concerned with maintenance
Is a director	Engages reflective practice management	Is a stage manager
Writes the script	Communicates meanings of the script	Follows the script
Challenges people	Channels challenges into morally fulfilling and productive programs	Keeps people happy
Has vision	Institutionalizes vision	Keeps lists, schedules, budgets
Exercises power of shared purpose	Enables power of professional and moral community	Exercises power of sanctions and rewards
Defines what is real as what is possible	Defines reality as what is possible for now, for our circumstances; tomorrow may be different	Defines what is real as what is
Motivates	Facilitates reflective practice	Controls
Inspires	Encourages	Fixes
Illuminates	Cheerleads; celebrates	Coordinates

commitment to deeply held human values that can be translated into farsighted educational programs and humane institutional structures. In the next chapter, I propose a theory of leadership for educational reform, a theory made up of leadership elements that relate to the reform agenda. Succeeding chapters will further translate elements of the theory.

Note

1. The following material has been adapted from the fifth edition of Thomas J. Sergiovanni and Robert J. Starratt's (1993) book on supervision, *Supervision: A Redefinition* (pp. 190-207). New York: McGraw-Hill.

❧ 2 ❧

A New Vision
and Theory of Leadership

In the last chapter, I suggested that the magnitude of school reform requires a leadership response from school principals. It is clear that the principal's leadership requires the development of a vision of what the school might become. *Vision.* There is that word. For some time now, we have been hearing about the importance of vision for leadership (Bennis & Nanus, 1985). As the word *vision* became accepted, its seemingly casual use rarely referred to a specific vision of something. Rather, vision was usually mentioned simply as something leaders should have. Often, vision seemed to be equated with goals. I think the word means more than the specificity implied in goals and more, certainly, than an empty slogan. By itself, however, vision suggests something disconnected from the realities of everyday life. To be important for principals, vision has to be connected to a more complex set of elements that constitute leadership. I suggest that vision is a dynamic source of leadership that imbues other aspects of leadership with a special energy and significance. To

13

understand vision, however, we have to see it in a larger theory of leadership.

A Theory of Leadership With Vision

In this and the next few chapters, I sketch a theory of leadership. Although I am concerned primarily with school principals' leadership, I believe that this theory applies to any educator who attempts to exercise leadership. It is important to note that I draw an ideal picture of leadership—what Weber called an *ideal type* (Eisenstadt, 1968). Probably no actual leader ever embodied all of these elements perfectly. The ideal may help to illuminate the exercise of leadership as it might be found in a variety of instances. A given example of leadership can be made intelligible when held up to the light of this theory. Usually, particular examples of leadership will exhibit greater strengths or emphases in one or more elements of the theory as well as other underdeveloped aspects. The theory can help us to determine whether in a given instance someone's leadership is broad or farsighted or rather quite limited in its scope.

My theory of leadership is made up of the following six elements. Although I have school principals in mind, I believe these elements apply generally to leaders in all areas of institutional life.

- Leadership is rooted in meaning—meanings that ground our identity as human beings, both individually and collectively; meanings that are the source for our deepest values.
- Leadership emerges out of a vision of what the leader and the colleagues can accomplish. The vision embraces an ideal, a dream that is grounded in those fundamental meanings and values that feed a sense of human fulfillment. The compelling power of leadership flows from a shared vision.
- Leadership is immersed in an awareness of drama, a sense of the importance and significance of what the members do or achieve, a sense of action charged with meaning and value, a heightened awareness of the heroic dimensions of the enterprise.
- Leadership involves a communal articulation of the vision that builds into a covenant, an articulation that captures the imagination and enthusiasm of the members, that encompasses their dreams and

aspirations and bonds their large collective beliefs into common agreements and celebrations.

- Leadership involves expressing the collective vision in institutional structures; institutionalizing the vision in the everyday life of the school; embedding the vision in the policies, programs, and procedures that channel the everyday energies of people in a common effort.
- Leadership requires the continuous renewal of the institution through everyday celebrations of the vision in ordinary and special activities, as well as through periodic restructuring of the vision.

This brief review of the theory of leadership unfolds in a more expansive treatment in subsequent chapters. For the moment, let us focus on the element of vision.

Expressing a Vision

People express their vision in a variety of ways. Some do it by telling a symbolic story, sometimes with mythical characters, sometimes with real characters. ("Our school should be like the school run by the three genial giants. One giant taught laughter, one taught forgiveness, and the other taught imagination.") Others express their vision in a series of abstract philosophical statements. ("Our school should stress functional literacy. That means literacy in our native tongue, literacy with computers, literacy between the sexes, literacy between ourselves and those we might go to war with.") Still others do it through a scenario of everyday events in the school or through describing two or three ideal teachers. (An ideal test in our school would look like. . . ." "Our kind of teacher mixes humor, firmness, caring, and intelligence into every class period.") For the more architecturally minded, the vision could be described through the shape of the building. ("Our school should have a learning laboratory connected to each classroom." "Our school would have no classrooms, only learning pods in a gigantic library stocked with wonderful and multitudinous resources.") For the engineers, the vision could be described in terms of structures and programs and systems. ("Our school would have continuous pupil progress contracts based on mastery learning and cooperative learning.") The more artistic will describe their vision with images and metaphors. ("Our school should be like a colorful garden . . ., a great symphony . . ., a treasure hunt . . ., a riverboat.")

However one formulates the vision, it is obvious that within each vision are assumptions and beliefs about the nature of learning, about the essence of being human, about the nature of human society, about the purpose of schooling. The leader dwells inside these beliefs and meanings, and calls attention to them through a vision statement.

One problem with discussing leadership is that we often focus primarily on the person or the position of the leader. In so doing, we tend to overemphasize the importance of personality characteristics, or talents like intelligence or decision-making brilliance, or the authority and power of the position the leader occupies. Obviously, the talents of the leader are important, and leaders need some position of visibility—not necessarily the top one—to be able to speak. The real source of the leader's power, however, is not in the leader's person or position; it is in the vision that attracts the commitment and enthusiasm of members. The point of leadership is not to get people to follow *me*; rather, the point is to get everyone jointly to pursue a dream, an idea, a value by which to make a contribution to the world and realize each person's highest human potential. Vision is essential for leadership; it is also essential for a followership—which includes the leader—of a magnificent quest.

Sources of Vision

A vision is usually formed by looking both inward and outward—looking inside the school at the people there and looking outside the school at the challenges society and individuals are facing, the challenges schools are supposed to prepare youngsters to deal with. Looking at the people in the school, the leader understands their absolute value. The leader realizes that all persons are sacred in their own right. People are subjects, not objects, and therefore should always be treated as ends in themselves, not as means to some organizational goal, whether that be the school's record on regional tests, the school's performance in sports, or the school's financial comfort—or, least of all, to make the principal's life easier.

Looking at the potential of all persons to become ever more fully human, to become more thoroughly *good* persons and to develop and exercise their talents and abilities more fully, the leader constantly communicates the respect and caring such people deserve. With that fundamental regard, the leader knows that the source of greatness in a school is in the teachers and the pupils. It is the leader's job to nurture their belief in themselves and in each other through a vision worthy of them. They are the fundamental energy for whatever human excellence the school achieves.

Looking outward, the leader tries to discern the challenges facing the individual person, the local community, and the larger society, especially in the approaching 21st century. The leader realizes that the school is supposed to help young people respond to these challenges in the present and in the future. Consequently, the leader's vision of the school contains an educationally appropriate response to those challenges.

Perhaps it will help us at this time to consider some of the challenges of the 21st century, to check out our own vision of what we are supposed to be doing in our schools. I discern the following general challenges to persons, and to local and wider communities. These challenges call out to educators to reconsider the substance and the process of schooling. These challenges call for a new vision of schooling.

Challenges for the Person

- Finding identity in relationship, in connectedness, rather than in isolated uniqueness
- Grounding self-esteem and self-fulfillment in giving rather than in possessing
- Gaining integrity through self-governance; overcoming passivity, conformity, alienation through being responsible for oneself and one's environment
- Honoring differences in a crowded world, rather than stereotyping and scapegoating

Challenges for the Community

- Finding a workable balance between environmental protection and an economy that supports necessary human services and quality of life
- Balancing the need for a private life with the need for widespread public involvement in community building, political processes, and democratic transformation of the social order
- Shaping education to fit a view of work as applying the mind and imagination to solving problems and projecting alternatives, and as service to the wider community, versus the view of work as labor, as a commodity, as a process of gaining status and power
- Building a national policy that balances international cooperation and national prosperity
- Understanding the postmodern challenge to take nothing for granted and accept that everything needs to be negotiated among all the parties involved

A thorough elaboration of these challenges would require several volumes and an understanding of the complexities of the future beyond my capacities. But these challenges are not plucked from the sky in an arbitrary flight of fancy; they are challenges we face now. Failure to resolve them is already causing serious personal, and political problems. John Gray (1995) sums up the situation:

> The ruling American culture of liberal individualism treats communal attachments and civic engagement as optional extras on a fixed menu of individual choice and market exchange. It has generated extraordinary technological and economic vitality against a background of vast social dislocation, urban desolation and middle-class impoverishment. (p. 25)

If we are to grow and develop as a people and as a nation during the coming decades, then we need to face these challenges more resolutely. Schools can no longer conduct business as usual, as though these challenges do not imply a thorough reassessment of the school as we know it. Some may want to rephrase the challenges to fit their own circumstances or to help formulate a vision. I do not mean to imply that these challenges require us to throw out everything that we are doing now. Rather, we must ask whether our present forms and the substance of schooling can be restructured and transformed to be more responsive.

Vision and Reflective Practice

Let us make an enormous leap and suppose that a school community has worked out a vision for the school; let us suppose that the principal has exercised genuine leadership in bringing about the completion of this task. Now, what is supposed to happen? Here is the vision; what's next? Let me suggest, for now, two ways leaders use the vision—by encouraging reflection and stimulating new efforts to express the vision.

Donald Schön (1983, 1987) has brought the term *reflective practice* into the language of educators (Sergiovanni, 1987). Reflective practice usually refers to the fact that professionals tend not to rely as much on theory and applications of theory as on intuition developed over years of experience in the profession. When asked to explain why they decided to do X rather than Y, practitioners tend to respond with hunches based on past experiences: "This looks like a case I had 6 months ago. Such and such seemed to work in that case, so I think I'll try it out here." Teachers behave similarly. They make many impromptu decisions during any given class in response to cues and clues provided by verbal and nonverbal language of students. Sergiovanni and Starratt (1993) liken the activity of teaching that is guided by these kinds of impromptu decisions to surfing. Surfers must constantly shift their weight and foot positions as they read the motion of the wave. Similarly teachers read the ebb and flow of student attention and energies and respond by shifting teaching activities. Similarly, when planning a curriculum unit, teachers intuit what will work best as a cluster of learning activities.

The literature suggests that professionals work more effectively the more they reflect on and monitor their actions. In other words, effective professional practitioners constantly monitor their actions, checking to see whether what they do is having the desired effect, and if not, changing to some other action. Such reflection tends to focus on the question, "Is this working?" or "What in this situation gives me a clue as to what will work?"

There is another kind of reflection, however, that relates more to our discussion on vision. That kind of reflection asks the question, "Why am I doing this?" or "What has this to do with where I want to go with this person?" In this kind of reflection, the professional practitioner is seeking to relate the present action to what it means, to its significance or value. Such reflection is intended to relate the present activity to those meanings embedded in one's vision to determine whether the activity expresses and is consistent with the vision. This kind of reflection brings questions of meaning and significance close to everyday actions. In so doing, the practitioner either alters the activity to make it more expressive of the vision or recognizes that the activity does indeed express the vision. In the latter case, the teacher would derive a deep sense of satisfaction that she or he is involved in that significant level of work called for by the vision. In their work on job enrichment, Hackman and Oldham (1976) discovered that knowing the significance of what one was doing increased the job satisfaction of people enormously, for it enhanced their feelings that they were doing something worthwhile.

The implication for leadership is that much of the leader's work involves asking the questions, "What does our practice of X have to do with our vision?" "What does doing Y tell us about the assumptions we make about children or about their ability to be self-directed learners?" "Why are we doing this rather than that?" Sometimes, the leader offers an interpretation of what she or he sees, such as, "I liked the way you encouraged the brighter kids to review the homework with the ones who were having difficulty. That helps the bright kids see how they can give back something to the school community." (That was part of a school vision statement.) That interpretation is also a form of commendation, another way of reinforcing the vision. Questions, interpretations, and commendations are ways the leader keeps the vision close to the action rather than in a book on a shelf in the principal's office.

Another way of bringing the vision close to the action is to challenge each teacher to come up with one new teaching-learning activity each month that expresses the vision of the school. Through faculty show-and-tell seminars, teachers can provide interesting examples of ways to put the vision into practice. In some instances, principals may give out awards for the best ideas—or even for the best ideas that failed. The point is to keep the vision close to the conscious, everyday awareness of the teachers, not as a formula of orthodoxy, but as a dream that is capable of taking many shapes and forms. As teachers become accustomed to designing learning activities that bring the school's vision into the classroom, they cannot help but become more enthusiastic stakeholders in the schoolwide enterprise. The point of this kind of reflective practice is to enable the vision to energize and lead the staff to transform the school into the kind of human learning community they want it to be. The leader facilitates the process. The staff and the pupils make it happen.

Summing Up

In these pages we have begun a voyage, attempting to chart the mysteries of leadership. The voyage continues through the next several chapters. By focusing first on the element of vision, we have been able to fathom some of the depths of that term and to discern the influence of vision on the life of the school.

Needless to say, each one of us has to see and to speak the unique vision possible for our school. Nevertheless, many common meanings and values are embedded in our separate visions, meanings, and values that we share as educators. Our stance toward life; toward the human adventure; toward the sacredness of children, of teachers, and indeed of ourselves; toward the beauty and majesty of nature; toward pain and toward evil and toward hope—all are shaped by our common human biography. As a community of educators, we are already blessed with a certain clarity about life's values.

Fashioning a vision of what our schools can be will emerge out of the many conversations we have had and will have, in the collective shaping of our journeys into words that hold that mystery, however incompletely. Hence, leaders above all others must be reflective, contemplative, meditative people. Our ability to hear legitimate echoes of our own journey in the words of our colleagues enables us to meld their expressions with our own into a perspective on our school that can guide all of us. To achieve that common vision means being open to using someone else's images and metaphors. Only the reflective leader who is close to the fundamental meanings and values that are rooted in her or his essential humanity will be able to hear others who use different languages express those same meanings and values, perhaps more richly and more profoundly.

⟨ 3 ⟩

Leadership and the Sense of Drama

In the last chapter, we considered the importance of vision for the exercise of leadership. The element of vision is situated in a larger theory of leadership in which besides holding a vision, a leader is seized by a sense of the drama inherent in the enterprise. That sense of drama involves grasping the significance of what the children and their teachers are or are not achieving—seeing their actions as charged with meanings and values. That sense of drama flows from those meanings and values essential to human life that ground the leader's vision of what the school can become. In this present chapter, we explore what that sense of drama might mean.

Forming a Character for the Drama

Leaders with a sense of drama are aware of the drama being played out in the lives of individuals. Individuals learn in schools to be a somebody or a nobody. They learn to be a nobody by experiencing ridicule, humiliation, and, most of all, indifference. After all, even the school problem-child is a somebody; everyone in the school knows who he or she is!

Every child has some talents. Schools, however, tend to value and reward only certain talents. Schools are not interested in cartoonists, gardeners, inventors, counselors, listeners, healers, prayers, mystics, basket weavers, mapmakers, salespersons, or preachers. It seems unimaginable that these kind of people might also come to appreciate geometry, poetry, history, biology, or that there might be a way to integrate geometry with cartooning, biology with gardening, history with healing, poetry with preaching. Many schools welcome only youngsters who can take directions, answer textbook questions, follow rules, and suppress spontaneity.

The leader with a sense of the drama being played out daily in the lives of children in the school knows that children are constantly making small, but cumulatively decisive, choices to be either a somebody or a nobody. People who eventually accept being a nobody sometimes literally kill themselves. More often, they choose subtler means of stopping living, whether by hating the world, constantly working at getting even, or burying their hurt in drugs or other opiates such as television and pornography. Or they may engage in denial in the form of compulsive consumption and possession as ways to guarantee that they are a somebody.

But a school can be an environment in which everyone becomes a somebody, in which everyone feels cherished and valued, in which everyone is seen as having something to contribute to the welfare of others. Every day schools help youngsters choose life or encourage them to choose death in the ways children are treated, in the reward structures of the school, in the ways curriculum is activated, and in what the curriculum emphasizes.

Although educators may not use the terms of life and death, their vision gives them a sense that there is a drama being played out in schools around the choices children make as they fashion themselves. Educators are aware that the school has inherited a script from the culture. The culture expects the school to teach the script. Yet within most cultures there is the realization that culture remains a living tissue only when it can be renewed by new voices, new visions, new perspectives. Thus, schools must simultaneously encourage a certain rewriting and improvisation while teaching the script.

Forming a character for the drama of living necessarily means choosing what scripts to present the character with; how much freedom to allow the character to improvise within the scripts; how much to encourage the character to define his or her own role in the drama; and, therefore, how much rewriting of the scripts will be possible. The costumes, scenery, and language for living at the personal and the public levels are human constructs. Either schools teach youngsters to shape those constructs to make their lives more human, or they teach them passively to follow the stage directions.

A generation ago, Robert Goldhammer (1969) poignantly captured the failure of schools to connect the curriculum to the life world of students:

> Is it conceivable that some direct relationship exists between the soaring incidence of sociopathic behavior, unsuccessful marriage, vocational dissatisfaction, and emotional collapse in our culture and the absence from the curriculum of any systematic treatment of love, intimacy, sex, feeling, fantasy, death, law, work, or real life? Or between the fact of my loneliness and the mystery of myself to me and the unmitigated absence of "me" as an object for explicit study in the curriculum?
>
> It is difficult to imagine how educational priorities that elevate penmanship to a realm of moral significance could ever have come into existence . . . while "me," through which all of my knowledge of the universe and of the dreams inside me is filtered and composed, was never a worthy enough subject to justify even a single course in human behavior. . . . It is difficult not to attribute at least some portion of my agony of self-ignorance, my uncertainty of who I am and how worthy, how powerful, how limited, how good, and how bad I am to the schools who had a hold on me for such a long time and who, in this context of knowledge, deprived me and betrayed me so completely. (pp. 28-29)

Schools need to teach that either we make the drama or the drama makes us; or perhaps that, paradoxically, we make the drama *while* the drama makes us. The drama of the drama is captured in the tension between the two creations. The struggle to emerge as a somebody from the trappings of costumes, poses, stock phrases, prefabricated opinions, and standard gestures is indeed a matter of life and death. One remains a cardboard character, a robot, a puppet, if all one can do is repeat what others have conditioned one to say. On the other hand, one cannot dispense with the linguistic and cultural conventions by which communication between disparate individuals is minimally possible. The key to this paradox is improvisation: One has to recreate one's character as one goes along, maintaining genuine spontaneity through being centered in the imagination of one's possibilities and the possibilities of circumstances. It is a risky business, to say the least. But freedom and creativity have always been considered suspect by the authorities.

Forming a People

The school's task in forming a people involves teaching the history of the people as that history influences and flows into the present. The history curriculum can bond individuals in the school into a sense of being a people through the heritage of song, poetry, art, heroic models, customs, and traditions. A people does not remain a unified social or political entity, however, unless the members are committed to renewing the drama inherent in overcoming and transcending the tensions such a unity implies. Youngsters do not learn how to participate in the drama of overcoming the centrifugal force of self-interest unless they learn the skills of participating in making the rules, negotiating disagreements, building a workable consensus through compromises, healing community wounds through reconciliation. In many large cities of the United States, where almost half the school population is made up of students for whom English is a second language, this concern with the drama of forming a people is perhaps more acute than anywhere else.

Forming Civil Society

Educational leaders with a sense of drama understand that beyond the drama of individual lives, public life is also a drama, and that schools—for better or for worse—play an important part in that drama. Beside the primary influence of parents, peers, and extended family, schools teach lifelong lessons. As a principal agency of the community, schools convey basic attitudes toward knowledge, work, self-esteem, public participation, social roles, and national values (Dreeben, 1968; Jackson, Boostrom, & Hansen, 1993).

For a variety of reasons, schools fail in some instances to encourage an active public life. Some people play their part in the public drama by being passive. Although they do what they are told, they are alienated by resentment, cynicism, or fear from the forces that control public life. Instead, they seek fulfillment through leisure-time recreation in their private, isolated lives. There is a script for that kind of drama, a script they learn at school, at home, and through the media. The script gives them lines such as, "Ah, c'mon, man, why make such a fuss about it? The people upstairs don't care what you think. You'll only get a bad name for complaining." In a brief clip on the evening news, one newscaster proclaims, "A government study shows that American workers continue to fall behind their Japanese and Korean counterparts. Commenting on the study, a member of Congress said the schools must teach better habits of hard work and obedience to authorities." A TV advertisement suggests, "Want to get away from it all? Fly Outback Airlines to the new Pineapple Taj Mahal Resort built on an island where the sun always shines and the service is only a snap of your fingers away." Textbooks teach the script more subtly by presenting history as a series of decisions made by government and political leaders, ignoring the telling of history from the bottom up, which might illustrate the hardships and the heroics of ordinary people.

Some schools enact the script by demanding passive intake and memorization of information, fostering habits of conformity, discouraging invention and curiosity, and punishing harmless expressions of individuality in costuming or coiffure. Some schools teach that social life in its present forms is fine and ought to remain fixed. Schools can teach school children both directly and indirectly that the status quo is justified by a kind of natural law social theory that communicates an ontological legitimacy to the present social order. In such a social order, people know their place, and the authorities know how to run things for the benefit of everyone. Order, predictability, and uniformity are supreme public virtues, virtues rewarded throughout the years in school.

For those youngsters on the bottom rung of the economic ladder, of course, the school tends to have little connection to the realities of life. For many of these youngsters, the scripts presented are foreign to their culture and demand such a complete abandoning of that culture that there is little but superficial parroting of the script at best, and, more often, a confused rejection. By the time these youngsters approach their teens, they are openly rebellious.

Schools can, on the other hand, teach youngsters responsibility for the direction of public life by teaching them the many ways they can be involved in fashioning the laws and policies that guide public life. They can also teach them to contribute to the quality of public life in their neighborhoods and towns through their own talents and commitments. Schools can teach that public life belongs to the public, and members of the public can shape public life through involvement in social, cultural, economic, and political processes. Schools can teach children about the world of public affairs, indicating how peoples and communities and individuals (who came from the same backgrounds as they) have made a difference. Schools can teach that public life is a drama where people find fulfillment in the struggle for community and moral purpose. Schools can teach youngsters that in public life they become a somebody or a nobody depending on how they take responsibility for themselves and their community.

Educational leaders with a vision know that schools are supposed to teach participation in public life. They have a sense of the vital importance of the school to their society: If schools fail to teach public responsibility and personal integrity, then the future of society is at risk. The day-to-day struggles of teachers to encourage youngsters to rise above selfishness express in a very real sense the struggle for the soul of the nation. No nation or people will ever achieve greatness without a generous sense of the res publica—public things—the republic . . . we, the people . . . this country, our homeland, our people. No people can form a fully human community unless the majority of individuals place the good of others before the good of themselves; unless they are willing to sacrifice some of their time, money, and special care for the homeless, the orphaned, the physically and mentally ill; unless they contribute some of their talent to improving the quality of public life for all. Educational leaders with a sense of historical drama know that, and they know what is at stake in the daily activities in their school.

Living the Drama of History

We are living in what most commentators call the postmodern world. The modern world, born more or less in the European Enlightenment, promoted values such as continuous social and economic progress; increased rationality in human affairs; scholarly advancement through the development of sophisticated scientific research; technological improvement of our standard of living through improved medical, psychological, commercial, and recreational services; the maximization of individual human freedom and individual human and civil rights; and the rationalization of the democratic state as the agent of the nation's destiny.

In the postmodern world, we have come to perceive the naïveté underlying these beliefs and values. Two world wars and countless regional wars have revealed the level of unspeakable brutality in the human psyche; police states engage in frightening physical and psychological torture; high-placed officials and business executives continually misuse their influence and power; and human beings seem as confused, addicted, angry, and mean-spirited as they ever were. Moreover, the advances of science and technology have not been an unmixed blessing. Industrial production and technological invention have literally made a mess of our environment, to the point where the survival of the ecosphere is called into question.

The motto of postmodern persons is, "Don't trust anything." By that is meant, don't trust scientists, politicians, corporate executives, church officials, salespeople, even your spouse. Certainly don't trust yourself, for you are more capable of deceiving yourself than anyone else is. Don't even trust the language you use, for it distorts as much as it reveals.

The postmodern sensibility can lead to three responses: to cynicism and despair, to a renewed sense of social Darwinism (the survival of the fittest, the smartest, the meanest), or to a search for a humbler grounding of human hope in a new understanding of who and what we are. I believe that the third choice is the only choice for educators. But it is a hard journey, a journey past broken dreams and broken selves. The journey into a humbler hope is illuminated by our understanding of the history of the modern age. Modern persons were led to believe that they were absolutely free to create themselves, to take from life's abundance whatever suited their purposes within a social contract that required only a minimum surrender of rights to ensure protection against the aggression of other isolated individuals. The modern age was the age of individualism. What the modern age did not understand was that the individual in isolation cannot become a fully human being.

The journey through the landscape of the postmodern world is a journey that communities must make, rather than a journey of isolated individuals. Guided by their collective memory of the mistakes of the modern world, communities can sustain the journey with compassion and gratitude for the gift of today. With the painful knowledge of the prevalence of human weakness, communities can promote forgiveness and the asking for forgiveness, and the understanding that both are among the primary presuppositions for social life. These are the lessons to be learned and taught by school communities.

Schools can teach the lessons from the premodern world, as well as from the modern world. The premodern world tended to suffocate the individuality of the vast majority of humans, who were thought to exist, by some divine right, for the pleasure of the monarchy, the aristocracy, and the hierarchy. It was that contempt for the great mass of humanity that brought about the overthrow of the ancient order of things, and led to the passionate glorification of the individuality of the common man (and, much more recently and provisionally, woman).

Equipped with the understanding that neither impersonal submersion into some larger social body, nor individual isolation from any social body, offers the proper model for our journey, schools can press on to explore our obligations to each other and to ourselves in our search for grace. Schools continue the journey also with the knowledge that reason and science alone cannot provide the guide to human destiny. Schools equip youngsters for the journey with the knowledge that our own propensity for evil bears watching, and the whole enterprise to build a new society that is more compassionate, more gentle, more in harmony with the rhythms and patterns of nature can collapse around us through deceit and fear and misunderstanding. School communities continue the journey teaching that there is not an iota of certainty to the outcome of our efforts; nothing can be taken for granted. Yet schools continue to offer hope that, working with the provisional nature of knowledge and with the fragile arrangements of our social life, a better history for humanity may yet prevail.

Hope From the Scientific Community

The hope of the postmodern learning community is sustained by a new convergence of thinking in the scientific community that humans are part of the natural environment, not separated from it as though living in another sphere. Modern biology and modern physics tell us that we are connected to the earth through an unseen, but nonetheless very real web of relationships. The food chain, the genetic chain, the electromagnetic field surrounding the globe, and the weather and ocean systems all work together and sustain our life. We belong to the earth much more than the earth belongs to us (Lovelock, 1979; Margulis & Sagan, 1986; Prigogine & Stengers, 1984; Scheff, 1990; Sheldrake, 1990; Turner, 1991; Zohar & Marshall, 1994).

Our sense of space and time tends to divide this relationship into segments with the spatial properties of size, edges, and insides and outsides and the properties of past, present, and future. But the reality, contemporary science tells us, is much more a totality, a simultaneous unity of time and space. We are one at this moment with the whole universe. Everything that is happening in the whole universe is affecting us and we it. In time, we are connected to everyone who has ever gone before us, to all that they learned, and to all that they accomplished. Being connected to the earth as it presently is, we are connected to the earth's history. We contain in our bodies right now all the microscopic footprints of the immense journey of nature and humanity up to this present moment. And we are connected also to the future, because pieces of what we have been and what we have said and thought and done will spin out through the future in the lives of those who come after us.

The problem with the modern person was that he thought—and this was an enterprise largely and intentionally restricted to males— he was orphaned. God, the cosmic clock maker, was out beyond the horizon. Having wound up the clock, He—also male—let it tick on under its own power and He disappeared over the horizon. The modern person saw himself standing alone against a cold and lifeless universe, having to make his mark on the universe on his own. A rather daunting challenge, but one, with the aid of reason and science, he thought he could take on.

Based on the view of human life emerging in contemporary science, schools can begin to teach that we are not called to be this superhuman competitor with the stars, always alienated and alienating, always calculating and computing, and always lonely. Rather our humanity is to be found precisely in being connected in space and time, connected to everything. Being connected to everything leads to a sense of reverence for all that sustains our life. Young people can learn that being connected in this way leads to a sense of responsibility to all that sustains us. This mind-set leads to affirmation of all the connections with the earth and with each other and our forebears through many forms of ritual and celebration.

Educators with this collective sense of the dramatic moment of history recognize that their task is to enable the younger generation to carry on the journey from the postmodern world to a new world order. The historical challenge to the younger generation of the transition between the postmodern world and the world of tomorrow requires a curriculum and a pedagogy for a new world order. That should be drama enough for any community of educators.

The Multiple Roles of the Principal

Within the drama of schooling, the principal can play multiple roles. On the one hand, the principal must be the overall director of the drama. The director has to know the script (in this case, a drama being carried on at the individual, social, and historical levels, where the resolution of the challenge at each level requires the resolution

on all levels—never a perfect resolution, to be sure). Any good director knows that her or his job is to keep the overall unity and focus of
the drama in mind and continually call the attention of the actors and
the support teams to that unity and focus. The director has to trust
the actors or players to interpret the script in such a way that it brings
out the essence of that drama through their own human artistry.

At other times, the principal has to play the part of the drama
critic, calling attention to an unacceptable performance, a distortion
of the plot, or a scene that defeats the whole production. Drama critics
also call attention to good performances—to a creative interpretation
of the script, a successful rewriting of the original script, and the
artistry of the support staff. A good critic cheers on the humanity of
the whole production. Principals can exercise their leadership very
effectively by being good critics of the drama.

Sometimes the principal is a drama coach, working among the
other drama coaches, the teachers, to refine a way of doing a scene
in the drama and suggesting new coaching strategies when the actors
miss the point behind the script. Or the principal arranges time for
the coaches to get together to discuss their coaching, to review how
the drama is going and make alterations in the script to make it work
better for the actors.

Finally, the principal must also be an authentic player in the
drama. Sometimes the bureaucratic drama of the school makes this
difficult. There are budgets to be administered, class schedules to be
coordinated, new textbooks to be reviewed, disputes over which
teacher has responsibility for the distribution of art supplies, and the
inevitable complaints against the principal's own shortcomings.
Often the bureaucratic script conflicts with the academic scripts of
teachers and parents. A parent complains that her daughter's class
schedule prevents her from taking an enrichment course in science.
A teacher who uses computers for teaching writing has been assigned
to a classroom without the proper electrical outlets.

The drama of schooling, however, is not simply a bureaucratic
drama, nor simply an academic drama, although it clearly is both of
those. It is also a drama of living, where characters encounter one
another to negotiate their relationships and their common tasks, to
deal with the mystery and the contradictions and the beauty and the
foolishness that make up human existence. When other people in the

drama perceive that the principal is playing an artificial role—that the person behind the role is hiding, or worse, is not even there—they will go into hiding themselves, and play behind their own artificial roles. The only way the drama can go forward is for people participating to have a sense that the true person of the leader is engaged, even while playing a role imposed by the bureaucratic or academic script.

It is at this level of engagement, I think, where the real drama in all our lives is being played out. It has to do with defining what makes up the rock-bottom foundation of being human, and once we are clear about that, then it involves building an environment that supports and nurtures being human to each other. What is becoming painfully apparent is that the world we live in doesn't bother to ask those difficult questions about how to live as a human being. We will see in a later chapter that those questions can and should become an integral part of the school curriculum.

To return to the principal who is called to be a player in the drama, her or his identity is not to be found in knowing all the answers, in standing above all the squabbles that go on every day in schools, in exercising the "science of school administration." Rather, the principal becomes a player by asserting his or her solidarity with all the human struggles to build an environment at the school that promotes the humanity of everyone. Everyone in that school is faced with the three choices left to the postmodern community: cynicism and despair, a new form of social Darwinism, or a search for a humbler human hope. Every day, the members of the school community face these choices anew. Insofar as the principal can by example invite them to search for hope through all the many small choices that they make, the principal enters into the drama as an heroic player, one who calls on the deepest and best sources of hope, which are still to be found in the players themselves.

Summing Up

I have suggested that leadership is fueled by a vision of possibilities. That vision leads to a sense of the drama being played out every day in the school. It is a drama of becoming a people, learning how to participate, how to negotiate, how to forgive, how to celebrate heroic ideals, how to give thanks for the planet that sustains us. Within that large drama is a play within the play—the drama of individuals struggling to be a somebody, learning about themselves through relationships, finding out how to be connected and at the same time to be an individual. The leader knows that he or she is also a player in this drama, knows that the script as presently written is a flawed script, one that often leads to tragic outcomes. Leaders know that is their responsibility—the whole company's responsibility, including director, coaches, actors, and critics—to rewrite the script so that the drama can be more humanly satisfying. Leaders know that the essence of education is the rewriting and the rehearsal of a new script. Their way of playing in the drama is to invite others to join in that task.

⤜ 4 ⤐

The Empowering Covenant

It is important to pause now and ask whether the picture we are painting is of a leader who is so strong as to leave others in the school no role beyond following the dictates of the all-knowing and all-powerful leader. The picture of leadership I present here is, make no mistake about it, a picture of a powerful person or persons. Leadership is powerful stuff; it has to be powerful to overcome the inertia of the status quo. It is important to remember, however, that the power of leaders comes from deeply held values, from strong convictions rooted in meanings essential to human life and critical in a particular historical and situated context for the betterment of human lives. These deeply held values and strong convictions bring leaders to see their circumstances in dramatic terms and their actions as weighted with significance. The power of the leader is not so much in the authority of her or his organizational position, but in the power of her or his ideas and dreams.

This initial picture of leadership can raise worries that I espouse a dressed-up version of the "great man" theory of leadership, a type of leadership that, although offering the possibility of engaging others in causes of high moral consequences, can and does more easily slip into a dictatorial, cultlike, and self-serving domination over others. Without toning down the power of leaders, the theory of leadership I propose expresses with equal force the need for leaders to bring their values and commitments to the stakeholders for discussion, debate, and the gradual development of a group commitment around commonly shared values and commitments. (Military leadership would include some of this but would obviously rely as well on a strict adherence to obedience to commands from above.) In other words, leadership takes place in something much closer to a community than to a bureaucracy. This leadership involves a common pursuit of ideas and ideals, not an overbearing imposition of the leader's exclusive ideas and ideals. Each community needs ideas and ideals that all can call their own, ideas and ideals that can energize the whole community into action. This is the reality I try to capture in the phrase *empowering covenant*.

An empowering covenant is the operative and express agreement that members of a community enter into to guide their activities and decisions. Originally, in Semitic cultures, a covenant signified a treaty between two unequal parties in which the more powerful party promised to protect the weaker party in return for service—a vassal treaty (Leon-Dufour, 1980, pp. 148-149). The term *covenant* took on a special tone for the Israelites of Biblical times, signifying the bond between Yahweh and the people of Israel (Anderson, 1962, p. 162). The term continued in use in Christianity and affected the way the early Pilgrims interpreted their destiny in their settlements in the Western Hemisphere.

I use the term *covenant* rather than *contract* because covenant connotes something sacred in the common life people share together, whereas contract connotes an agreement between two self-interested parties. A covenant implies deeply held values and commitments; a contract refers to quid pro quo, an arrangement whereby I get something in return for giving something.

Covenant is also a term with an elastic meaning. Some covenants are more sacred than others; some are limited or temporary. The relationship between a lawyer and a client is considered a covenant, but it is usually temporary. The relationship between a mother and her child is considered a more lasting covenant. The covenant between a teacher and the school community is not as sacred nor as permanent as the covenant between a parent and a child. In using the term *covenant* in this context, I intend to signify a strong bond among members of a school community (especially among the adult educators in that community) that is woven of the ideals and ideas they have agreed to pursue. In most schools, contract rather than covenant better describes the relationship between the teacher and the school community. Where one finds more of a covenantal relationship among members of a school community, one finds an exceptional school.

The covenant I refer to is an empowering covenant. By that I mean three things: (a) Each person finds a personally fulfilling way of exercising his or her unique talents in the pursuit of common ideas and ideals, (b) members of the community are able to achieve things together that they could not achieve on their own, and (c) the power of the ideas and ideals raises people's abilities to a new level and gives a focus and an intensity to their activities that they would not have without those ideas and ideals. I elaborate on each of these below.

What Is Power?

For many people, the term *power* has negative overtones. It is associated with force, coercion, threat, and sometimes violence. Power is often viewed as something only a few people have; "the powerful" are thought to control or unduly influence the affairs of the community. From that vantage point, empowering people implies that those who hold power over others *give* away some of their power. Yet the reality is that no one has power over another without that person's consent. If everyone refuses to comply with those "in power," then those persons have no power. We saw that happen not long ago in Eastern Europe. Even the power of persuasion implies that the listener assents to the reasonableness of the speaker's argument. The power of the judge to impose a prison sentence is based on an assumed prior agreement of the people to live according to the law.

Instead of thinking about power as meaning power *over* someone or something, we can view power as something each person possesses: power to be and do. The most interesting power each one of us possesses is the power to be ourselves. No one else has the power to be me. Only I can be me. Often, I fail to use that power and instead try to live up to an idea that others have of me or to some collective image of what the truly modern, sophisticated, cosmopolitan, urbane man should be.

We are all socialized, to one degree or another, to displace what we want to be or do in order to conform to social norms of propriety and tradition. "Good boys" don't do that! "Good girls" would never dream of doing that! "At Saint Viator's School, we simply don't do things like that." We grow up maintaining our fragile sense of self-esteem by what we think others think of us. Fear of disapproval often leads to a suppression of being or doing what our spontaneous wishes suggest.

What "growing up" means, however, is that we learn how to be ourselves and still live, more or less, within the acceptable bounds of social propriety and tradition. Maturity means taking responsibility for ourselves, being the person we want to be, and loving the person we are. It means deciding to resist the fads and trends of popular culture when they start to twist what we value. When our own sense of integrity is at stake, we are able to risk the disapproval of others. In other words, each of us has the power to say yes or no. That power may be heavily circumscribed in certain situations, as in conditions of severe poverty and oppression, but it is a power we never lose. Although we turn it over to other people, it always belongs to us, and we can take it back when we choose. It is the power of freedom, the freedom especially to be myself, to sing my own song, dance my own dance, speak my own poetry—the freedom to be true to my best self.

The paradox about this power is that although it is mine, it is given me for the benefit of the community. I can only exercise the power to be me in relationship to my community. Some mistakenly think that the power to be an individual is a power *against* the community, a power to use the community for selfish purposes or undermine the community in pursuit of purely personal goals. That attitude leads to a kind of narcissistic, selfish isolation. That form of self-centeredness is actually self-destructive. I can be myself only in relation to others, other selves whom I value as they value me. I can only express myself in relation to the world, to another person, to a particular circumstance that at that moment is part of my definition (such as my home, my workplace, my neighborhood, my garden). I express myself by responding to persons and events in my immediate surroundings, and that expression is an expression either of giving or of taking, of gratitude or of greed, of celebration or complaint, an affirmation of life or a denial of life. Insofar as my expression of myself is giving, thankful, celebratory, and affirming, I myself receive life, I grow, I am nurtured. Insofar as my expression of myself is taking, hoarding, complaining, and denying, I hurt myself and those around me. The self I express in negativity is an expression of self-destruction.

The power to be myself is a remarkable power. It can be an enormously creative power—a power to create myself, so to speak, while adding to the life around me. It can also be an enormously destructive power, a power to destroy myself (even though that takes place by barely perceptible, minuscule choices) while smothering and depressing life around me. Some people choose not to exercise the power at all because they sense the existential risk involved. Better to leave the choices in the hands of others; let them decide for me what kind of person I should be.

Empowerment as Personal and Professional Fulfillment

When we speak of empowerment, we should distinguish between the process of empowerment and the achievement of empowerment. Just as with the word *liberation*, there are two meanings: One deals with the activities one engages in to liberate oneself while one is not yet liberated; the other meaning signifies that one has reached the state of liberation. Empowerment in a school context is a relational process in which administrators and teachers engage in a mutual process of surfacing what the power to be and the power to do means in this particular school, what positive qualities are attached to the exercise of that power, and what limitations are imposed by the circumstances of the communal effort at schooling. Empowerment is not a process of administrators giving power to teachers. Rather, it is a process that involves mutual respect, dialogue, and invitation; it implies recognition that each person enjoys talents, competencies, and potentials that can be exercised in responsible and creative ways within the school setting for the benefit of children and youth.

Empowerment can also be an achievement. It can be arriving at a state of autonomy in the exercise of one's power to be and to teach, using all the talents and wisdom at one's disposal. As an achievement, empowerment is always relative, for as was implied earlier, we never exhaust the possibilities of our power to be a teacher. What empowerment means as a policy, then, is a commitment that the school environment continually nurture teachers' growth in their abilities to promote the growth of students, both through their own modeling of what it means to be an authentic person and through their engagement with the students and the learning material itself.

Empowerment has to happen with each individual teacher. Each teacher must be invited to be authentically herself or himself. Sometimes that invitation will be very direct, as in the case of the principal who asks, "What would you like to explore in your work as a teacher?" or "What do you need to do better that you already do well?" Sometimes that invitation will be indirect, as when teachers are asked for suggestions for next year's staff development days. Sometimes the invitation will simply be an attentive ear when a teacher needs to discuss a problematic situation at the school.

Empowerment has to be individualized. Although all teachers may be invited to develop new skills, such as using computers in classroom instruction or developing debate formats within classrooms, each teacher should be expected to bring his or her own creative insight and intuition to the exercise of those generic skills.

Empowerment as an essential element of leadership means recognizing the power all persons—teachers and students—have to be themselves. It means inviting them to exercise that power with joy and laughter, responsibility and compassion: joy, because the exercise of this freedom brings profound satisfaction; laughter, because in the exercise of individuality we often catch ourselves acting absurdly or foolishly; responsibility, because in the act of being myself, I have to honor the relationships that tie me to the community; and compassion, because the exercise of individuality can sometimes lead to mistakes, excesses, and misunderstandings. The expectation that forgiveness is an everyday necessity is a precondition for any communal exercise of our power to be ourselves. Married people should understand that, perhaps, best of all.

A fundamental prerequisite for any effort at empowerment is trust. If a teacher is to feel free enough to try out more spontaneous activities, he or she must trust that there is room for mistakes, that differences will be tolerated, and that unique insights will be honored. Most teachers have been socialized into relatively limited protocols of teaching. They have not been encouraged to go beyond the textbook and the curriculum guide to think for themselves and design creative student learning activities. They have to know that they are trusted to try out new possibilities in a responsible and effective manner. If they have learned to expect immediate criticism of deviations from standard operating procedures, they will not risk trying something new.

The presence or absence of trust is often the critical feature of a school's culture. Fullan (1991) correctly cautions school leaders to reculture before they restructure. He also cautions about premature attempts to create a vision before people have been invited to a more participatory involvement in shared governance (Fullan, 1993). Invitations to a more personal involvement in the life of the school—a consistent pattern of invitation to share ideas and proposals about major directions the school should be taking—have to be seen as the groundwork for creating a culture of participation. The empowerment of the individual that this culture implies is essential to the development of a shared sense of leadership and responsibility for setting the school moving toward renewal.

Administrators are not aware of how critical this sense of trust is. Telling teachers to trust simply doesn't work. Trust is something built up over time through the personal relationship an administrator is able to establish with each teacher, through constantly telling the truth, through encouraging the sharing of ideas and criticisms, and through acting on the suggestions of teachers. When sufficient trust is established, teachers believe that administrators' talk about increased teacher autonomy and creativity is genuine.

Empowerment of a Community

Empowerment on an individual basis is only a small part of the empowerment agenda. Empowerment must be felt and exercised by the whole staff. When individual teachers who feel empowered work together to respond to school needs, empowerment is qualitatively raised to a new strength. An empowered staff comes to believe that it has within its ranks enough talent and insight to respond to most school problems and create an outstanding school. By discussing ideas, sharing experiments, and pooling resources, an empowered staff can generate extraordinary energy and enthusiasm. That should be the ultimate goal of any policy of empowerment. When an administrator has nurtured that kind of empowerment, then the whole staff becomes involved in the exercise of leadership. Through the united efforts of such a staff, sharing of visions can result in an overarching vision for the school; mutual problem solving and organizational evaluations can lead to structural redesign and institutional transformation. That in turn leads the staff to a greater sense of empowerment, more confidence in their own creative talents, and an increased willingness to pursue the dream of creating an exciting and satisfying school.

From this vantage point, one can view empowerment as a genuine exercise of self-governance and moral fulfillment. One of the goals of leadership, it seems to me, is to have a community take charge of its destiny, and in so doing to find the profoundly satisfying experience of creating something wonderful. Every teacher worthy of the title dreams of a school environment where youngsters find learning an exciting and awe-filled experience. That is the ideal we all hold out for ourselves. Empowering teachers to work collectively toward that goal is what leadership is all about.

Empowering Ideas and Ideals

The third kind of empowerment, the power of ideals and ideas to lift the community to new levels of performance, is tied to both individual and communal empowerment. When a leader or group of leaders involve the community in discussions of a vision of what they want the school to become, they begin to tap into enormous sources of energy and enthusiasm. As members of a school community begin to frame a vision for their school, they develop a shared sense of the significance of what they are doing and a shared appreciation of the potential that they possess collectively to turn the school into a place of excitement and achievement.

The power of a shared vision fuels the teachers' deepening involvement with the complexity and reach of professional competency. It deepens their willingness to explore new or more effective responses to student learning through their own action research and participation in professional development workshops. It deepens their commitment to the success of all children. Their shared vision creates not only a bond between the teachers, it bonds them more closely to the children. It leads them to empower their students. Their shared vision gives a focus and intensity to their work and provides the confidence that when they work together, they can solve the problems and overcome the obstacles involved in student learning. In short, the covenant of shared ideals and ideas embodied in a shared vision empowers teachers. It elevates the teachers to higher and personally and professionally fulfilling levels of performance, which in turn raise student performance to higher levels.

It becomes clear how inextricably the leader's development of a shared vision is connected to empowerment. Empowerment cannot be seen as an opportunistic add-on. Rather, it is absolutely essential to the leader's effectiveness. Through the power of everyone—power enriched and energized by the passion of the common dream—the school community can move forward. This power grows by the joys of small victories; by the sense of being involved in a shared enterprise; and by the feeling that a problem encountered is not my problem to solve alone, but our problem to solve together.

Organizing for Empowerment

The kind of empowerment I seek does not take place simply by wishing for it. As was implied earlier, the culture of the school must be an empowering culture with supportive organizational patterns. Besides personal involvement of the principal with individual teachers, structural arrangements have to be in place. Empowerment themes must be tied to teacher appraisal and instructional supervision. A variety of award and recognition schemes need to be in place so that different talents and initiatives can be honored. Other structural arrangements can include a weekly and monthly schedule that allows for a wide variety and frequency of small-group staff workshops and seminars, perhaps a design studio with computers and visual media to design new curricular units, perhaps retreat opportunities where teachers can explore the appropriate integration of their life stories with their teaching.

Schools and school systems are notoriously impoverished environments. Some administrators expect teachers to be empowered because of a circulated photocopy of a speech about it. Empowering teachers, however, requires schools to enrich their environments with opportunities for empowerment, to make the place of work so exciting and full of ideas and stimulating discussions of new possibilities that it would be impossible not to grow. Administrators sometimes blame teachers for becoming stale after their first few years of teaching. That is to blame the victim for a disempowering environment that smothers enthusiasm in routine and punishes inventiveness in subtle demands for conformity and uniformity.

Summing Up

In the past few chapters, I have attempted to construct a complex and enriched view of educational leadership. We have seen that leadership involves vision, a sense of drama, and the humanly demanding effort of empowerment. These elements all go together. A vision helps to empower; empowerment enriches the vision; entering into the drama of living encourages seeking the power to be oneself, to own one's unique name; and individual empowerment provides the foundation for communal empowerment that in turn enables the whole staff to enter the drama of institutional transformation under the guidance of the energizing vision. The quest for institutional transformation leads to the next chapter, where we explore another piece in the puzzle of educational leadership.

⋞ 5 ⋟

Leadership and
Institutional Transformation

In previous chapters, we have looked at the leader's vision, the leader's dramatic sense, and the leader's shaping of an empowering covenant around the vision. It is important to remember that these views of leadership reflect an ideal of leadership. All of us in varying ways and degrees try to express that kind of leadership, but we also know how often we settle for good old mindless, authoritarian, manipulative, sloppy, defensive, expedient administration. Studies of decision making in organizations have shown how seldom administrators approach the norm of rationality assumed for good management (Lindblom, 1959). Schools, like most organizations, lurch and zigzag forward by what Lindblom (1959) calls a "disjointed incrementalism"—that is, they make a series of small decisions that have very little to do with one another, but result in changes that enable the organization to muddle through until the next crisis. In our more candid moments, most of us admit to similar practices. Nevertheless, we often try to raise our sights, shake off the opium of routine, grasp

47

the challenges in front of us, and ask ourselves whether things might be different at our school.

At this point, we may understand the importance of having a vision of the school's possibilities and of entering into the drama of life at our school. Having those insights won't do us a bit of good, however, unless we know how to operationalize them—put them into some consistent pattern of action. In what follows, I explore what I call institutional transformation.

The Paradox of Institutional Life

Max Weber believed that institutions in the modern age are both the biggest threat to human freedom and creativity and the only sphere for the exercise of human freedom and creativity (Eisenstadt, 1968). Institutional life is governed by routines, roles, rules, policies, guidelines, and standard operating procedures. The intent of these structural characteristics of institutional life is to make everything as predictable as possible. If everything is uniform and predictable, then the institution will know what it is doing and how to do it most effectively. In the process of imposing uniformity and control, however, the institution suppresses creativity and freedom. Creative fire drills are not allowed in schools. Pupils are not free to write poetry on math exams. Teachers are not free to teach whatever strikes their fancy; there is a syllabus that must be followed. Schools must test all children on the same criteria; otherwise, how can the children be compared and labeled as smart or dumb?

Institutional life is also where things get done in the modern world. To be sure, there are a few people like Picasso who appear to embody the ultimate free and creative person. Yet even a Picasso must be connected to institutions such as suppliers of paints and brushes, art dealers, banks, art galleries, and so forth. Picassos cannot show their art without the organizational supports such as art galleries, newspaper announcements, and museums and other organizations to buy sculptures. For most of us, the only arena for productive work is within an institution.

Weber was getting at something rather more subtle (Eisenstadt, 1968). For him, the truly creative act was to *change and transform* the institution. The decision to assert authentic freedom is in opposing the institution, getting it to change its ways, bringing it to face a new direction. Institutional life will always impose limitations on creativity and freedom because of limitations in resources and limitations in institutional mission. But institutions are also sources of power and influence and productivity. Harnessing that power, influence, and productivity in the pursuit of an exciting and ennobling goal is indeed an expression of freedom and creativity.

The implications for educational leadership are clear. Inviting the staff to take up the work of institutional transformation is to offer them a genuine expression of their freedom and creativity. Moreover, the goal of the transformation is to create an environment that itself promotes freedom and creativity among the youngsters we educate. At the same time, we must not be naive about the task at hand. Institutional transformation is not a project for a year's enthusiasm. It is the work of at least a decade, if not of a lifetime.

In our highly mobile society, administrators move from school to school every 4 or 5 years in a pattern we call career advancement. We need to rethink our time frames for the principalship if we are serious about reconstituting our schools. Institutional transformation does not happen in 1 year or in 3 years. The investment by human beings in such an enterprise has to respect patterns of human growth and institutional trial and error that simply take a lot more time. Politicians want quick results so they can be reelected. But only superficial results—or perhaps it would be better to say superficial subterfuge—can be accomplished in short time frames, unless, of course, the government is willing to quadruple the resources of money, staff, and support material for schools. Even dramatic increases in material support cannot shortcut the need for thinking, discussion, design, and redesign.

To transform our schools, we need to have some idea of what makes them work, how they are put together. We need to understand the structural dynamics of schools so that the transformation goes beyond the surface, beyond posters in the corridors and a rousing speech at graduation.

A Model
for Schools as Institutions

I find it helpful to view institutional life as an onion with several layers (Sergiovanni & Starratt, 1993). When we go into a school, we see children moving from one part of the building to another, teachers standing in front of classrooms writing on the blackboard, principals standing in the corridors directing traffic, librarians scowling at the youngsters giggling in the corner. That is the outer layer of the onion, what I call the operational level (see Figure 5.1). Beneath that layer is what I call the level of organization. This layer is made up of the budget, the class schedule, the allocation of teachers to classes, the calendar of the week and the year, the assignment of teachers to school yard supervision, the schedule of staff meetings, and so forth. The level of organization is the blueprint for distributing resources such as time and space, money and people.

Third is the level of programs. Here we find the educational work separated into programs, each with its own rationale, its curricular scope and sequence, its ways of assessing student learning, its use of instructional materials. The program level is related to the curriculum and to the syllabus, but it also includes the counseling program, the athletic and other co-curricular programs, and parent programs. Beneath it, we find the level of policy. At this level, the school structures the ways it will accept students, grade them, promote and graduate them, discipline them, communicate with parents, hire and fire staff, activate due process proceedings with students and staff, provide for staff participation in decisions, negotiate contract disputes, and so on. The level of policy sets those large guidelines that tend to define the identity and character of the school on a day-to-day basis.

Continuing our examination of the onion, we find at the next level the institution's goals and purposes. It is at this level that the school sets its mission and defines its purpose. The level of goals and purposes is like a compass by which a school knows where it is going. These purposes are translated into more specific goals such as "to ground the students' verbal expression in acceptable grammatical and stylistic principles."

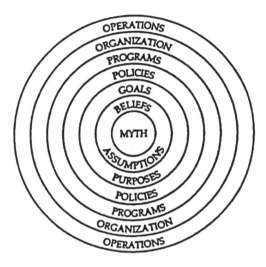

Figure 5.1. The School as an Onion

Next comes the level of beliefs, values, and assumptions. School people rarely explore this level of their institutional life; beliefs, values, and assumptions tend to go unquestioned. Beliefs, values, and assumptions, however, are to an organization what solar energy is to photosynthesis: They fuel the whole enterprise; they energize the other levels of the institution. Beliefs, values, and assumptions are extremely difficult to change; they give the institution its character and its culture. They can, however, be surfaced and articulated. Often, when a school has to write out its philosophy, these beliefs, values, and assumptions get expressed—at least the more positive, publicly approvable ones. There may be class, race, and gender assumptions and ideologies that no one surfaces for public scrutiny.

Finally, at the core of the institution, we find its myths. By myths, I do not mean childish fantasies. Rather, I mean those deep assumptions about the nature of reality itself. Here we find the myths and meanings by which people make sense out of their lives, by which they define value and judge human striving and place themselves in a definable order of things. Myths are almost inaccessible in everyday life, because they function at such a basic, taken-for-granted level of our awareness. Yet they constitute our whole fabric of the intelligibility of the world. Philosophers and anthropologists and artists might rummage around in that core of myth and meaning, but most people live their lives in quiet confidence that life holds together and that the circumstances of their lives have some kind of ultimate meaning. Nevertheless, it is in that core of myth, meaning, and belief that leaders find the grounding for their vision of what the school might and ought to become. At the core one finds myths of heroism, of human destiny, of the sacred nature of all life. One finds myths about humans' relation to nature, about the values underlying the nation's identity, about those virtues considered to be the crown of our humanity. At the core, too, one finds myths about the nature of human society, about the source of order in the universe, about the large meanings one finds in human history. Those myths are usually embodied in story, in poems, and in highly symbolic literature. They shape our convictions, our beliefs, and our attitudes toward most things. Because of shared myths, we can reach consensus with others on our beliefs and assumptions.

Science, for example, is based on a myth, namely, that there is order rather than total randomness in the universe. Without that myth (which can never be scientifically proved), the activity of scientists to map the order of the universe would be meaningless. That is one of the myths that sustains educators, as well. Another myth that sustains educators, one that goes back at least as far as Socrates, is that if we know the good and the beautiful, we will choose the good and the beautiful. I proposed earlier the myth that as educators we are involved in a drama and that schooling is a way to learn how to make the drama work for us and others.

As indicated in Figure 5.2, there can be schools in which those deep meanings are seldom referred to and the core might just as well be empty because of the total focus on the surface tasks in the school. In Figure 5.3, we see a school where the myths and beliefs at the core of the school, articulated in a vision, interpenetrate every layer of the onion. In every program and policy, we would find reference to a core of meanings that unify and provide identity to the community.

In my earlier remarks on leadership, I mentioned the leader's sense of the purpose of a school and how that was made up of learnings about fundamental values in life. Those learnings are grounded

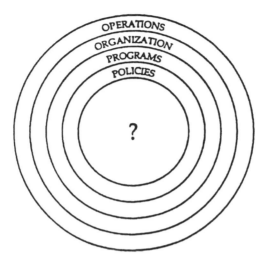

OPERATIONS
ORGANIZATION
PROGRAMS
POLICIES

?

Figure 5.2. A School With No Sense of Vision or Core Purpose

in myths about our communal destiny, our identity as a nation, our relationship to nature, and so forth. Often, leaders express their sense of purpose in a more metaphorical vision statement. In the vision, the leader suggests what the school can become, what ideal values it can embody. A vision statement is often more powerful than a purpose statement because it employs imagery that touches the heart as well as the mind. Vision statements employ elements of myth because they express deep human aspirations in poetic imagery. We sometimes hear educators say, "Our classrooms are like gardens." "In our class, we compose a symphony of joyful music." "This school is like being on a journey." "We voyage into the unknown on the fragile bark of science." "Sycamore School is like a family." "We are a learning community." "Our school is America in search of its identity." "Our school is a rehearsal for the drama of life." "Here we are quite clear that we are on a quest for the holy grail."

A vision statement can never be put into a logical argument. It points to something profound and ineffable, yet it is intuitively grasped as containing something close to the essence of the school. The vision is not a full-blown philosophy statement or a long-range plan. It is not a developed blueprint; rather, it is a symbolic compass,

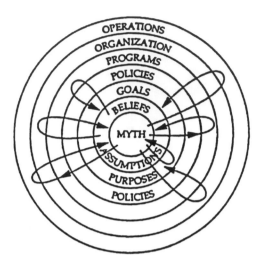

Figure 5.3. A School Energized by Its Vision and Beliefs

pointing in a direction toward an ideal. Much of its power comes from capturing three or four central meanings that are open to multiple applications and representations within the school. The vision statement creates a value framework that enables daily, routine activities to take on a special meaning and significance, making the school a special place and instilling feelings of ownership, identity, participation, and moral fulfillment. Leadership becomes management by meaning. Peter Block (1987) offers an interesting tip about vision statements: If your vision statement sounds like Motherhood and Apple Pie and is somewhat embarrassing, you are on the right track!

A vision statement does not impact student learning unless it is institutionalized in the various layers of the school life. One of the reasons why schools remain dysfunctional is that the community fails to confront the organizational structures and dynamics that create the dysfunction. The onion model is one heuristic tool for helping to identify structural sources of contradiction to the vision and a framework for building a school whose vision is integrated into the total fabric of the school as an institution. In healthy schools, the layers of the onion are consistent with one another; each expresses

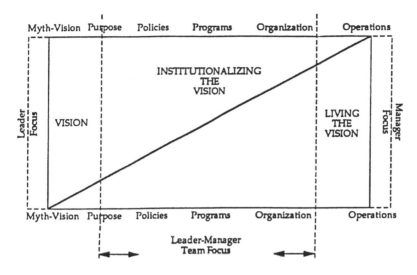

Figure 5.4. The Work of Restructuring/Renewal

what is implied in the layer below. The policies of the school ought to be consistent with the purposes of the school; the programs of the school ought to be consistent with the policies and the purposes of the school; the allocation of space and time and other resources ought to be consistent with the rationale behind the programs of the school; and so forth.

This linking of the operational and organizational levels of the school with the deeper core of purposes, beliefs, and myths helps us to see why leaders and administrators need each other. Whereas leaders may tend to focus on the vision, administrators are the ones who know how to make things work.

Teaming Up
Leadership With Administration

Recasting our onion into a two-dimensional figure (see Figure 5.4) helps to show where the talents of leaders and the talents of administrators tend to divide. Administrators tend to focus more on the operational edge of the school. Leaders feel more comfortable at the vision edge of the school. To institutionalize the vision, both need to work together in the middle parts of the figure, which is where the vision is translated into institutional reality. Leaders and administrators have to collaborate to clothe the vision with policies, programs, and organizational structures. Administrators are relatively comfortable manipulating variables in organizational structures and programs, but they need the leader to talk through the implications of the vision at a level of specificity sufficient for them to fashion institutional forms of the vision. This view of leadership may seem rather ambitious and idealized, but it provides a framework by which principals can wear both hats, that of leader and that of administrator.

Finally, Table 5.1 shows the entire flow of leadership activity, moving from rooting the school's vision in myth and meanings to the shared expression of the vision of the school that leads to a more formal expression in a mission statement. The vision and mission create the empowering covenant that energizes day-to-day work. The development of the empowering covenant provides the groundwork for translating the vision into institutional form as expressed in policies, programs, and standard operating procedures. These institutionalized forms become operationalized by specific teachers and students going about their work on a typical school day. Thus, we see the elements of the framework of leadership building on one another until they issue in the renewal of the school in its day-to-day life.

The final element of leadership has to do with the ongoing rejuvenation of the vision through celebration and continuing efforts to embed the vision more clearly in the institutional forms of the school. A primary responsibility of the leader is to see that the core of the onion—the myths, beliefs, and purposes—suffuses all the other institutional layers of the school. One of the dangers in an institution is that everything gradually becomes rationalized. Means become fitted to ends in ever tighter logic that ends with excluding consideration of alternatives. After a while, the institution becomes so rationalized that there is no room for imagination.

Core myths and beliefs are not about logic; they are about life. The leader calls attention to the life-giving core by asking outrageous questions such as these:

Table 5.1 Integration of the Vision With the Various Levels of the Organization of the School

Roots of the Vision	Articulation of the Vision		Institutionalization of the Vision	Operationalization of the Vision
Meaning Associated With	*Beliefs About*	*Formal Statement of the Mission of the School*	*Formal Organization*	*Woodrow Wilson School*
Human destiny	The human mind and how one knows	Cultural purposes	Policies	A school with
The nature of the individual	How children develop as full human beings	Political purposes	Programs	—People coming and going to classes
The nature of human society	How children should be socialized	Academic purposes	Procedures	—Activities
View of the past and of the future	Varieties of learning	Moral purposes	—Graduation requirements	—Interactions making up a fabric of experience
	Moral values	Economic purposes	—Curriculum	—Meanings
	Political values	Social purposes	—Course selection and assignment	—Patterns
	Spiritual values		—Grading criteria	—Rituals
Frequently embedded in imagery, metaphor, myth, and story	What kind of future the young will face	*Processes of Communicating the Vision*	—Discipline	—Symbolic action
			—Student activities	—Celebration
		Empowerment covenant	—Staffing	
		Thematic purposing	—Budget	
		Rituals		
		Celebrations	*Informal Organization*	
		Championing		
		Heroes	Community spirit	
		Rewards	Style of communications	
			Tone of relationships	
			Informal group	
			Informal curriculum	
MYTH	ASSUMPTIONS, BELIEFS	GOALS, OBJECTIVES	POLICIES, PROGRAMS, STRUCTURES	OPERATIONS

- Is there enough poetry in our policies?
- Does our daily and weekly timetable allow for, nay, encourage a time for communal singing?
- Can we stop the relentless sequence in our lesson plans for a moment of play or healing?
- Are there moments of Mardi Gras every month when we can put on funny costumes to ridicule the routine masquerade of everyday life?
- Do we relieve the tedium of spelling drills, worksheets, tests, and reports with mystery stories, magicians' tricks, fantasy adventures, treasure hunts, puppet shows, and folk dancing?
- Is the life of learning so relentlessly boring that we know no moments of surprise, awe, wonder, laughter, or delight?
- Where will our inventors and artisans come from if in our school we have no time for making things with our hands or wondering about patterns and forms that take shape as we invent something new?
- How can we ever foster the habit of contemplation or reflection if we never take time to simply look at something, to marvel at its intricacy, to learn to know it in all its subtle patterns, to revere life's fragility in a butterfly or a buttercup?
- Have we no time to learn the art of negotiating, the craft of conflict resolution, the caring of listening, the grace of forgiving?
- When are we supposed to confront bias and inequity and injustice in our world? When will we discuss new possibilities in public life?

The response, of course, to all these questions is, "There is no money in the budget for it; it is not on the final exam; we have to cover the syllabus; we have not got the time today; the parents will think it's too frivolous; there is nothing in the research literature on this." Only when the leader shakes the school out of its tendency toward organizational rigidity can the daily operation of the school begin to resemble what was intended in its vision.

Summing Up

In presenting this framework for principal leadership, I have attempted to lay out what I consider the bare essentials of leadership. These leadership elements show a dynamic kind of interconnectedness; they interpenetrate one another and need one another. To be sure, the picture of leadership I present is indeed an ideal. The ideal, however, provides us a way of looking at present practice and understanding what is missing. It also provides us with an understanding of the kind of people we should be looking for in school principals.

In these chapters, I wanted to suggest three things about educational leadership. First, as Weber suggests, the work of institutional transformation is among the most significant and heroic things human beings in the modern world can do with their lives (Eisenstadt, 1968). Second, the work of institutional transformation begins at the level of myth, belief, assumption, and mission. It is at this level, I maintain, that we are most challenged by the potentialities of the 21st-century world. A revitalized sense of meaning, purpose, and direction at the core of a school will energize the transformation of the school at all other levels. Principals, individually and collectively, must address this starting point of renewal. Third, institutional transformation takes a long time and a continuing commitment to the task. It requires considerable technical, administrative, and planning skills. And more than anything, it takes the courage to embrace the long journey.

Many principals may say that the task is too much for them. Indeed, the task is too much for any one individual to sustain. Alone, no one can assume the burden of institutional transformation. Paradoxically, however, all that we know about successful changes in schools points to the individual school as the locus of change. Because schools differ in so many ways, the transfer of change from one school to another rarely succeeds, and then only when the second school adapts the change to suit its own environment.

Principals must seek support from local and state educational officials for the local autonomy to pursue restructuring within broad state guidelines. Likewise, principals must join hands with teachers and parents and call out the best in them. Further, principals need support mechanisms within the school and external networks with other principals who are attempting to transform their schools into vibrant communities of adventurers and explorers of the possible. Principals need to sit down with other principals and discuss their dreams and frustrations, laugh at the foolishness, and weep over the nastiness of everyday experience. Being able to share with others experiencing similar struggles and small victories will enable them to put their work in perspective and to go back to it with hope.

⋹ 6 ⋺

Leadership and Reflective Practice

In the previous chapters, I sketched an ambitious view of the leadership of the school principal. The same generalizations could be made for educational leaders in other positions, including teachers, superintendents, and state education officials. I focus on the principal because I believe that the individual school site is the locus for significant transformation of the educational system, and for that transformation to take place the principal's leadership has to call forth the leadership of the teaching faculty, of the parents, and indeed, of the students.

Some might argue that my view of leadership is too ambitious, too demanding, and too idealized. My response is that leadership in education today is indeed demanding. The job of transforming U.S. schools into vibrant learning communities that prepare all youngsters—including the physically challenged, so-called at-risk children, so-called average students, and so-called talented or exceptional students—for productive, fulfilling, and flexible citizenship in the 21st century is not a job for the faint-hearted or for unimaginative bureaucrats. The job requires that educators rethink what schools should be from top to bottom and then take that clarified vision to the parents and the community and argue for its realization. The work of rebuilding the school to embody the vision will require years of continuous effort. To propose that all this be accomplished by the same methods with which schools have traditionally been managed is to misjudge the enormity of the task of school transformation for the 21st century.

Ongoing Renewal of the Vision

The last element of leadership that I mentioned in the overview of leadership in Chapter 2—"Leadership requires the continuous renewal of the institution through everyday celebrations of the vision in ordinary and special activities, as well as through periodic restructuring of the vision"—is sometimes omitted in treatments of leadership. Once the leader has brought about the initial embodiment of the vision in the institutional structures and processes of the school, most people consider the leader's job completed. Yet a moment's reflection would remind most people with experience of organizational life that no vision is ever fully realized in institutional life. Not only that, a vision that has been institutionalized rapidly becomes the new orthodoxy, and its institutional expression becomes as rigid as the previous orthodoxies it replaced. Leaders will be challenged to keep the institutional arrangements flexible and responsive to the internal and external dynamics of the school. The leader's job is by no means ended when the initial restructuring of the school has taken place.

Furthermore, the whole view of change has changed. No longer is change viewed as a time of turmoil and inventiveness between long periods of stability and predictability (Fullan, 1993). Change is seen now as the only thing that *is* predictable. With this as the new definition of the status quo, Senge (1990) reminds us that for organizations to remain effective in the turmoil of rapidly fluctuating expectations and demands, they must be *learning organizations*. They must constantly nurture learning about new developments in their environments, study how to improve their technology and their service, and reflect on the nature of what their members believe they are supposed to be doing and to what purpose. Senge (1990) calls our attention to a role of leadership necessary for any self-renewing organization, and that is the role of teacher. Leaders in self-renewing organizations teach, not so much by lecturing as by calling attention to what the ongoing learning agenda is for all the members and by pointing to issues that require clarification, problems that need to be renamed, and new frameworks that realign old cause-and-effect patterns. Such a leader-teacher reminds the members of the school community that the work of the school is complex, multidimensional, and dynamic and, therefore, they will never find a way of operating that even approaches perfection for more than a day. The life of the school and the lives of the students are affected by constantly shifting variables in the external and internal environments, such as new state mandates, new demands on limited school budgets, new members on the schoolboard, broken marriages, bankrupted or downsizing businesses, economic recessions, flare-ups of old community antagonisms, new research that suggests a different approach to instruction, shifting populations in the catchment area, more accessible data banks for student learning. A seemingly infinite list of variables requires that educators continually be learning, adjusting, realigning, and inventing (Stacey, 1992).

This situation suggests that educational communities have to seek simultaneously for stability amid turmoil and inventive adaptability and flexibility to remain responsive to the dynamic internal and external environment of the school. Educational leaders need to find that stability in a clear sense of purpose and vision, and they need to build in flexibility in the way they name what is problematic. This suggests for me a broader understanding of the term reflective practitioner.

The Reflective Practitioner

Donald Schön (1983) introduced the term *reflective practice* into organizational studies as a way of overcoming the apparent dichotomy between theory and practice. He found in his research that professionals did not deduce solutions to problems of practice from theories they learned in graduate or professional schools. Most of the time, they confronted uniqueness in any given problem in front of them (which never conformed to the model problems taught in the university). Problems faced in practice always involved far more contextual variables than the reduced variables of the theories and models studied in schools. For doctors, the patients' illnesses are complicated by age, gender, influence of other physical ailments and medications being taken for them, occupation, family stress, and family history of health and disease. Architects and engineers have to deal with contextual variables such as climate, land contours, properties of various materials under varying climatic conditions, costs, aesthetics, and environmental impact.

The Bounded Rationality of Organizations

Administrators in all kinds of organizations, including schools, have been known to eschew theory. Besides the research by Lindblom (1959), Simon (1945), and March and Simon (1958), which pointed out the limited rationality that goes into most managerial decisions, Peters and Waterman (1982) point out the desirability of *not* spending much time in rational analysis before risking a decision. They espouse a theory of "ready, fire, aim," which means that organizations operating in a dynamic and turbulent environment learn where they are going by intense involvement in projects with a clear, albeit limited focus. Out of that project and others like it will come a greater sense of the larger vision of where the organization should be going.

Fullan (1993), I think, overemphasizes the point that vision and mission statements always come *after* activities that mobilize people in collaborative experiments. It is true that in many instances, people have to learn to work together, how to develop the habit of collaboration, and how to achieve small success in limited projects. He seems to present the work of visioning, however, as a top-down process motivated by a desire to control and predict the future. It seems to me that the activity of visioning is never finished, but that it starts with a view, however limited, of *a* direction to move in. The vision will indeed be fleshed out and modified as people work together in addressing the particulars of the work in front of them, but the work of visioning requires a periodic pause, a lifting of the head above the immediacy of the work, and a concentration on those ideas and ideals that capture where the people want to go. Louis and Miles (1990) seem to strike a nice balance in their analysis:

> The organization can cycle back and forth between efforts to gain normative consensus about what it may become, to plan strategies for getting there, and to carry out decentralized incremental experimentation that harnesses the creativity of all members to the change effort. (p. 193)

The Craft Nature of Professional Work

Blumberg (1989), among others, has helped us appreciate that professional work involves certain craft elements. Just as a craftsperson adjusts to variables in the materials being worked on and to the interests and circumstances of the client who might have commissioned the work, professionals also rarely handle a situation in exactly the same fashion as they handled similar situations the day before. Minute differences in contextual variables alter or nuance the response. Intuitions gained through experience come into play. Improvisation is more the rule, rather than uniform rational logic. But it is the improvisation of the expert, not of the untrained. Improvisation seems to involve a kind of instantaneous reflective process in which the craftsperson is simultaneously performer and critic. As the craft work unfolds, the flowing reflection on the work keeps pace and continually suggests tiny adjustments to make the activity more precisely productive of the intended effect. There is also reflection after the work is finished, as the craftsperson studies the finished work. This reflection enables the craftsperson to take note of the form embedded in the material and how that form found expression under the craftsperson's creative manipulation. The reflective craftsperson is also able to see defects that might have been avoided if alterations were made earlier in the production.

Reflective Practice

Studies of professional practice seem to indicate that reflection is at the heart of professional practice. Practitioners who analyze the uniqueness of a problem confronting them, frame the problem in ways that structure its intelligibility, think about the results of their actions, and puzzle out why things worked and why they did not tend to build up a reservoir of insights and intuitions that they can call upon as they go about their work. Not only do they reflect after the fact, but they bring this reflection to bear on the problem at hand. As Schön (1983) points out, they carry on a conversation with the problem and listen to it talk back. They are reflecting even in the moment of action so they can respond to the action as it unfolds. Reflective practice is based on the assumption that the script for the interaction is, at best, only partially written. It will be completed on the spot as the interlude unfolds.

Expanding the Notion of Reflective Practice

I suggest that the notion of reflective practice needs to be expanded to meet the need both for stability as well as adaptiveness in the work of successful principals. Reflection on the intelligibility, significance, and value of the activities of the educational community provides a stable place in the midst of the noisy immediacy of organizational work. As principals and teachers engage in the day-to-day effort to "manage messes" and solve the countless crises that emerge during the normal school week, they need to have a sense of what they are about and what it is they are trying to accomplish. Without that sense of the intelligibility behind their choices, they can be so swept up in instinctive reactions to problems that they end up increasing the problems and adding to their burden of stress. More often than not, a sense of being centered, of being focused, is not something that they are consciously aware of; it is something habitually beneath the surface of their decisions and responses. Yet it has to be surfaced from time to time to restore the sense of stability amid the turmoil of daily activity and provide motivation to energies that are overtaxed.

The Reflective Community

Whereas Schön (1983) tended to focus on the individual profes-sional and his or her reflective practice, I believe that our under-standing of leadership and change has deepened to the point where we realize that the reflection has to take place with others more often than by oneself. One of the marks of a leader, then, is the continuous invitation to groups, and, indeed, to the whole school community, to reflect on what they are doing. The goal of this continuous invitation is the reflective community. In the context of the school, this means that the teaching faculty would be growing in their ability to reflect together on what they are doing. It also means that the teachers would be inviting the students to engage in the same kind of reflec-tion as an *integral* part of *their* learning.

I outline three ways of doing collaborative reflective practice, based on suggestions to individual practitioners: (a) problem nam-ing, (b) educational platform, and (c) double-loop learning. If we keep in mind the earlier discussion of the principal as a player, a coach, and a critic in the schooling of drama (Chapter 5), these ele-ments of problem naming, educational platform, and double-loop learning, now seen as a collaborative activity, take on a new light, viewed against the human drama of the school.

Problem Naming

Studies of the decisions of practitioners have noted how the nam-ing of the problem influences the entire problem-solving process (McPherson, Crowson, & Pitner, 1989). Sometimes, the problem is incorrectly named. Sometimes, the problem is susceptible to being given several names. Suppose a student is sent to the principal's office for repeatedly failing to turn in her homework assignments. The problem could be called disobedience; it could be called laziness; it could be called not having a place at home to do the homework. The problem might be that the student can't do the homework be-cause she has a learning disability not previously diagnosed. The problem might be that the student is being abused by her parents at home and is too emotionally distraught to concentrate on schoolwork. It could be a combination of factors. We cannot address the student's problem until we have identified and named what the real, not just the apparent, problem is. That is why some prefer the label *problem finding* to problem naming; it stresses the probing that must go on to find the real problem.

An unreflecting practitioner names problems according to the familiar and superficial. Frequently, the problem carries overtones of being a problem for *me* until I remove it somehow. That response often leads to the most expedient solution, which is no solution at all, but simply a removal of the problem from my awareness. In the example of the young girl brought to the office for repeated failures to do homework, the principal could scold the girl and threaten punishment if she does not start turning in her homework and send her back to class. If there is a serious problem at home that is causing the girl's inability to do her homework, this action by the principal would not solve the problem. But it could make the principal feel as though he has solved it. At the least, it has removed the girl from being a problem to the principal. His action, however, may cause an additional problem by inducing the girl to copy a friend's homework to avoid being punished by the principal, thus leading her into the habit of cheating.

In many cities of the United States, the central-city schools are populated by minorities, mostly Asian, African, Caribbean, and Hispanic Americans from families living below the poverty line. In those communities, almost all of the economically successful families have moved out. The environment in which those central-city children grow up contains many examples of despair, hopelessness, welfare, and crime. Some observers of life in the inner-city claim that the customary rite of passage for the boys is to go to prison; for the girls it is to have a baby. Yet some reformers call for longer school days and a longer school year, tougher promotion standards, and more required subjects. Those central-city students are already reading 3 to 5 years behind their suburban counterparts; the school drop-out rate is three to five times higher; and the absentee rate and class cutting are out of control. Have the reformers named the problem correctly? Are their solutions to the problem at all helpful? There is some evidence that the reforms suggested would actually increase the number of school dropouts.

One of the standard errors in problem naming is to mistake the symptom for the underlying cause. We are confronted by an angry parent and we think the problem is her anger. The parent accuses a teacher of bias against her child, and we think that shifting the child to another teacher will solve the problem. By taking the time to find out what the problem is, however, we may find that the decline in the youngster's grades has to do with his need for glasses, or that the boy's grades had only fallen by a fraction and the mother was blowing the decline all out of proportion. It may turn out that the boy has become involved with a local soccer team and is not spending as much time on his studies as before, but socially he is maturing because of the experience of making the team.

Sometimes, the problem is the result of an emotional flare-up and really requires no action other than patience and forbearance. At other times, the problem may be much deeper, such as a disagreement between two teachers over promotional policies. Again, the crucial procedure is to keep exploring why this is a problem. Only when we have identified the problem underneath the problem and named it so that all the participants in the problem can agree on what the problem truly is can we begin to explore an appropriate solution. Sometimes, the solution involves dealing with the immediate problem as a first step and setting up a series of actions to deal with underlying causes over the next few weeks or months.

When we think about the word *reflective* we recognize that it means to re-flex, that is, to bend back upon. In problem naming, we try to look back over the problem to see it in a context, as part of a larger whole or pattern. When we name the problem, we are abstracting from the immediacy of the details of the problem and seeing it in its structural aspects, that is, as fitting one or more categories by which we can analyze its basic meaning. So we ask, "Is this a political problem, an emotional problem, a definitional problem, a policy problem, a resource problem, a cultural problem, a bias problem, a technical problem, a budgetary problem, and so on?" Sometimes, we may not be able to name the problem in any meaningful way. In that case, the best response is to do nothing. Look concerned, perhaps, but do nothing. Instead of attempting inappropriate solutions, we should insist that people closest to the problem come to some agreement about the nature of the problem.

As Schön (1983) indicates, our experience will aid us considerably in our efforts to name problems accurately. Most on-the-job learning involves trial and error. Error can be a great teacher. When we see a problem that we tried to solve in a certain way in the past and remember that our solution blew up in our face, that experience should cause us to be cautious about trying the same solution again. The experience might lead us to consider whether we had named the problem accurately in the first place. Frequently, without thinking much about it, we get a hunch about the nature of the problem. That hunch may come to us because over the years we have encountered similar problems and now can spot them more easily.

The stress on experience is important because in the practice of problem naming, others may provide more insightful reflections on the problems due to their more extensive experience. The collective experience, and hence the collective wisdom of the group, can far surpass what any individual is able to bring to the problem-naming process. Also, when other people are involved in the naming of a problem, they will tend to take more responsibility for trying solutions. The community of educators is, after all, collectively what educates the child, rather than this or that teacher.

Teachers, in turn, need to assist children in the process of problem naming. Clearly, this can be a part of the academic agenda, a process of bringing youngsters to exercise higher-order thinking skills. In historical studies, for example, teachers can ask students to name the underlying problem behind a conflict between nations or religious groups. In literature studies, teachers can ask youngsters to name the problem confronting the hero of the story. Beyond that, teachers can ask youngsters to reflect on their own experience and ask them whether they ever experienced a problem like the one under discussion.

Beyond the conceptualization of problems in various subject matter classes, teachers can also facilitate problem naming in other areas of the students' lives. Problems like loneliness, conflict with authority, ethnic identity, and group conformity make up the terrain of growing up that youngsters must traverse. Naming problems and searching for healthy responses to them can and should be part of the school's curriculum. Normally, this kind of teaching and learning goes on informally between teachers and students. There are times, however, when it can be appropriate to engage the students in group discussions of these problems. Indeed, there are times when these problems need to be named in conversations with individual and groups of parents.

The principal and other leaders within the faculty need to take the problem-naming process a step further, however. The next step is to ask whether the solutions or responses to the problem are consistent with the vision or mission of the school. In this way, the community can look for consistency in its decisions. Community members can see that they move toward their vision of what the school can become by linking that vision to their responses to everyday problems. This kind of consistency can lead to an awareness that there are structural changes needed at the school. There may be a set of problems that are, in fact, institutionally generated problems. Group reflection on the problems in the light of the school vision may illuminate the institutional source and lead to a restructuring of that institutional dysfunction. In any event, the principal's attention to the relationship between problem responses and the vision is one way of continually bringing the vision before the community in its efforts at ongoing renewal.

Educational Platform

A second important element in reflective practice is what I call the *educational platform* (Sergiovanni & Starratt, 1993). Political parties have what they call a platform. The elements of a political platform indicate the fundamental beliefs and actions that are supposed to guide the decisions of the party when in office. Platforms can also be statements of priorities or significant goals the party wants to achieve. One's educational platform is something like that. It comprises fundamental beliefs about human development, the nature of learning, and the relationship between schooling and adult life in society. Often, one's platform is framed as a balance between discipline and creativity, between conformity to rules and personal autonomy, between social and academic learning, and between required and enrichment subjects.

From the previous discussion of the leader's vision for the school, we can see that the platform would be those beliefs and values that support the vision; some would say the elements of the platform make up the roots of the vision. Vision is distinguished from platform mainly in that the vision is a reaching out for something not yet realized. The platform can refer to beliefs that support what is or beliefs that drive the vision. In distinguishing between administration and leadership, we can say that leaders have a vision, and administrators have a management agenda. Both leaders and administrators, however, need to act out of a set of beliefs and values, and these are what make up their platforms.

As Schön (1983) found in his research on professional practitioners, their platforms tend not to be expressed in formal statements. Rather, one infers their platform from their actions. Earlier research by Argyris and Schön (1974) revealed that frequently administrators had two platforms, one that they would express when asked to articulate their beliefs about how to treat people and how to run an organization, and another that was expressed in their actions and decisions. Frequently, the platform-in-action was not the same as the espoused platform; often, the actions contradicted the words. Most administrators express a platform of individual care and attention to teachers and students, yet in practice that platform yields to decisions based on expediency due to the daily pressures of time, politics, money, and exhaustion.

Remembering that reflective practice is something that needs to be done collaboratively, the principal should work toward a schoolwide platform. Principals should encourage the teachers to write out platforms and compare them among themselves to see where they agree and disagree. Such an exercise might be the focus for an inservice day or faculty retreat. The goal of the discussions would be to form consensus around a schoolwide platform.

Many educators find the exercise of writing out their educational platform rather difficult. Because they have never done this task before, some need some categories to guide their first attempts. About 10 categories are sufficient to get started. Categories such as the following may be useful:

- The three most important aims of education for youngsters in our school are . . .
- Students learn best (when, through, in) . . .

- The social significance of learning is . . .
- The most valuable elements of the school curriculum are . . .
- A teacher is . . .
- The best kind of teaching is . . .
- The preferred kind of student-teacher relationship is . . .
- Classroom learning ought to emphasize . . .
- The preferred kind of school climate is . . .
- The overall purpose of my work is . . .

After the teachers have written a first draft of their own platform, they share that with other teachers. By comparing and contrasting platforms, ideas will be sharpened and modified until the teachers become reasonably comfortable with one statement. Where there are irreconcilable differences between groups of teachers, they may agree to disagree for the moment. The principal or a consultant should subsequently try to offer a larger framework that would allow those conflicting beliefs to coexist.

Copies of the platform or brief phrases from the platform can be posted in several places to serve as reminders of what the faculty believes in. They can also serve as invitations to individual teachers to take a moment to reflect on the consistency between their platform-in-action and the espoused platform. Some educators take 1 hour a month to review their past performance in light of their platform and preview upcoming decisions in the light of their platform. Others ask a trusted member of the staff to provide periodic feedback on their behavior seen from the standpoint of their espoused platform. All of these activities serve to get the community to be more reflective about its practice.

The teachers, in turn, should get students in their classes to compose their educational platforms and post a composite class platform on the door of their classroom. Teachers can then refer to that platform as situations arise in class. Thus, reflective learning is enhanced for the students. Teachers who work at getting the students to reflect tend to learn in a new way the value of reflection for themselves. Again, the platform is a way for the principal to keep the assumptions and beliefs behind the vision close to the surface of everyday life at the school.

Double-Loop Learning

Another element in the reflective practice of successful professionals is their ability to engage in what Argyris (1977) calls *double-loop learning.* Double-loop learning is contrasted with single-loop learning. In single-loop learning, one sizes up a situation or a problem, makes a decision, takes action, and then evaluates whether the action or decision led to the expected result. If the results were as expected, then the single-loop learning stops there. If the results were unexpected, in single-loop learning, one proceeds to try another decision, take another action, and evaluate the result. In double-loop learning, one tries to get on top, so to speak, of the situation and observe what is happening, observing his or her own behavior as well as that of the other people in the situation and looking at the structural properties and underlying dynamics of the situation. In double-loop learning one seeks to learn *why* certain choices work and why others do not. Single-loop learning tends to be satisfied with the knowledge that some things work and others do not. Double-loop learning tries to find out why. Through double-loop reflection, one looks at the inner dynamics of encounters and not simply at the surface; one tends to function with an awareness of the multiple perspectives that lend meaning to human actions.

Principals who are double-loop learners will be more alert to the broader contexts of their everyday actions. For example, they may be talking to a ninth-grade math teacher and simultaneously attend to the larger context that includes the following factors: This is a second-year, ninth-grade math teacher whose evaluation reports from her department chair at the end of her first year were negative; her tenure approval hinges on showing improvement this year; her math supervisor doesn't know anything about coaching inexperienced teachers; and the local teacher union leadership is watching the case carefully due to past failures of the school to assist inexperienced teachers.

Such principals are much more conscious that they not only want to help this teacher, but the future level of cooperation of the union may hinge on their skill in handling this teacher. They are aware of their own feelings—that they need to win this one. Their feelings also caution them to balance the need to be fair and helpful to this teacher with their responsibility to the schoolchildren to weed out incompetent teachers.

This example shows reflective practitioners in action. While interacting with a teacher, they are simultaneously observing the action as though from a distance, reflecting on the various levels of significance embedded in this interaction and feeding those observations back into the interaction with the teacher. Note that the principals are aware of some elements in their own platform, namely to be fair and helpful to teachers and provide the best teachers for the students. Somehow they must create a win-win result in which the teacher wins, the students win, the principal wins, and the unions win. They want to avoid a situation where one party wins at the expense of another party. Aware of the multiple stakes involved, they are more likely to steer the situation so that it does not degenerate into a win-lose situation; they will be able to honor all of their values and not be forced to surrender one to preserve another.

Another result of double-loop learning is the awareness of our ability to deceive ourselves, to rationalize, to be self-serving, and to use other people. All human beings strive to protect themselves from negative judgments of other people, exercising a variety of defensive strategies to minimize damage to their self-esteem. The double-loop learner is more sensitive to the need to create win-win situations. We win not by making others lose but by helping others win.

The reflective principal will take double-loop learning one step farther. The principal will coach the teachers, either directly or through the use of a consultant, in the practice of double-loop learning. In groups, teachers will practice describing a problem and analyzing the larger context of the problem and the underlying dynamics at play. They could begin with any of a number of problems at the school, looking at the multicultural dynamics at play or examining implications for the parents, the teachers' union, the budget, or the politics of the schoolboard. Thus, they will come to better understand that school problems are nested in a complex web of relationships. Although a decision may favor one person or group over others, double-loop learning will lead the problem solvers to attempt to minimize the negative impact on those others.

A principal, attempting to keep the vision of what the school can become close to the everyday choices people make, will insist that one of the outer loops in double-loop learning is the vision. As the community or groups in the school community tackle a problem, they will have to include the vision as one of the contextual factors that needs to be taken into account. They may have to make an expedient decision that ignores the direction the vision suggests they should go, but at least they are conscious that they are making that choice.

Summing Up

The three elements of reflective practice discussed in this chapter go together. All three contribute to the community members' ability to make sense out of the challenges and situations they face on the job. All three elements are ways of making meaning, ways of understanding, and ways of putting one's intentions into action. All three forms of reflective practice actually make up a single complex form of reflective practice. Problem naming renders the problem intelligible. The platform enables one to follow consistent values and bring meanings and values to an otherwise undifferentiated parade of characters demanding attention. Double-loop learning enables one to attend to one's platform and to the multiform levels of meaning to be found in most encounters. All three individually are examples of reflection in action. When all three are linked together in consistent patterns of reflective practice, it is easy to see how each one complements and strengthens the other two.

We can see that the leadership of the principal who attempts to engage the community in the continuous celebration and renewal of the vision is related to the building of a reflective community of learners. The continuous invitation to reflection provides stability for practitioners whose days are filled with unpredictability and complexity. By relating these three forms of reflective practice to the vision, the principal is able to keep the vision at the center of the everyday activities of the school.

❧ 7 ❧

Education as Personal Formation

Plots, Players, and Possibilities

In the next two chapters, I continue the treatment of educational leadership by focusing on two core ideas in an educational leader's vision, namely, the human person and the kind of society human persons sustain. This focus can help us see what we are doing, why we are doing it, and how we might do it better—all essential components of a vision of education.

In this chapter, I consider the work of education as *personal formation.* Some may immediately object, assuming that I refer to the formation of the child by the teacher. On the contrary, I refer to the formation by the youngster of his or her own life. This formation occurs under a variety of influences and within a variety of communities. Schools are supposed to be places where the educating influences enable youngsters to self-consciously, or intentionally, sculpt their own lives. The educating community organizes and sequences many learning experiences that provide enriched opportunities for intense and prolonged self-formation. But I am jumping ahead of myself. To situate what I mean by personal formation, it may help to review some competing points of view.

Personal formation has been considered an essential element of education from the time of the ancient Greeks to the present. The precise nature of personal formation, however, has always been a source of debate. In the United States, that debate has taken on fresh contours in response to societal contexts and shifts in schools of thought about moral and personal growth.

The exclusively instrumental emphasis in schooling on preparation for work and career in a rapidly changing and increasingly competitive world is being challenged by calls for a balance between the vocational and the social and intellectual goals of schooling (Wirth, 1992). Voices are raised in government and other sectors of society that schools should be nurturing attitudes and understandings about responsible citizenship and healthy personal development, as well as promoting lifelong learning for its own sake (Purpel & Shapiro, 1985; Starratt, 1990). The increasingly multicultural fabric of society and the problems of urban poverty, crime, and environmental preservation, to mention a few elements of the social context of schooling, require attention in schools as much as preparation for the world of work.

At the same time, the debate over methods and pedagogies has heated up among educational theorists, learning psychologists, and ethicists. Some would have schools strengthen their systems of rewards and sanctions in a more focused effort at character formation (Lickona, 1989). Others promote values clarification or debate over moral dilemmas to develop insight and understanding in a society of pluralistic views about morality and ethics (Kohlberg, 1981b). Some stress the teaching and understanding of moral principles (Peters, 1966). Others stress the principles of caring and the demands of relationships (MacMurray, 1961; Noddings, 1984). Still others encourage critical reflection on power relationships, conditions of communication, and a praxis of self-emancipation (Giroux, 1988; McLaren, 1991).

I have found the use of perspectives derived from the metaphors of drama helpful in analyzing personal formation in schools. Three questions arise to reframe the debate:

- What are the various plots in the drama of personal formation?
- Who are the players in the drama of personal formation?
- What are the possibilities for the drama of personal formation?

Exploring our responses to these questions may generate fresh insights and possibilities for our vision of schooling.

The Plots

There are a variety of renditions of the plot of personal formation in schools: (a) the social contract version, (b) the intellectual version, (c) the accommodation version, (d) the ideological version, and (e) the reproduction version. Each presents a one-sided approach to education as personal formation and generates problems that call for critique. In this section, I address each in turn and conclude with my own version of the plot, in which I attempt to be more faithful to the essentially dramatic nature of personal formation.

The Social Contract Version

In the social contract view of personal formation, children (especially boys) are seen mainly as young savages: impulsive, cruel, self-centered, physically overanimated, sexually overstimulated. Placed in the orderly environment of a school, they learn by trial and error, crime and punishment, habituation to routine and good manners, exposure to good example, and unremitting moral advice of people in authority. After 6 to 8 years of this regimen, the children emerge tamed, well-mannered, socialized, and responsible members of society. They have learned to restrain their selfish natures in return for the social guarantees of acceptance and livelihood.

This version of personal formation, obviously derived from the social philosopher Thomas Hobbes, is consistent with a rather negative view of the human person as intrinsically selfish and aggressive, requiring external controls to keep the individual's behavior within socially agreed upon boundaries. In its pure form, this plot of personal formation functions with extrinsic controls and sanctions, rigorously and consistently applied, as the proper pedagogy of personal formation to mold habits of restraint and a self-interested awareness that the social contract works in each person's interest. The plot is not altogether misguided, for it is true that part of the socialization of the young involves restraining antisocial impulses and instilling habits of restraint on self-centered behavior.

In a more balanced rendition, the social contract plot presents personal formation as molding virtue as well as curbing vice. Beginning with external rewards and punishments, youngsters gradually learn to internalize the traditions, social routines, and moral principles that society requires for the carrying on of common public life.

Even in this more balanced rendition, however, the socialization of the young into acceptable social behavior presents problems. Ernest Becker (1971) argues that from infancy into young adulthood, young people constantly learn to *displace themselves* in the socialization process. By that, he means that in order to feel acceptable to others, they learn to do what others want them to do rather than what they might spontaneously do. In the process, youngsters learn to place the source of their self-esteem in the approval of others rather than in a sense of their own abilities or worth.

But if socialization requires the displacement of self, and if in the process of personal formation teachers are in effect socializing youngsters into the forms of traditionally acceptable behavior, are the teachers not perpetrating a crime against these youngsters in encouraging them to surrender their sense of themselves to the good opinion of the authorities? Does this not lead eventually to the formation of hollow people, devoid of inner conviction, dependent on the judgment of others, lacking integrity and autonomy? Make no mistake about it, teachers are involved in this ambiguous enterprise. What is needed is a socialization process that promotes integrity and autonomy as well as an acceptance of common norms of social behavior.

The solution may be to help youngsters understand why certain behaviors are deemed unacceptable by society. By explaining the reciprocities required for social life, the rights and duties that impinge on all members of society, teachers can enable youngsters to acquire a sense of the intelligibility behind social norms and customs. Youngsters also need to understand the fabricated nature of social conventions, especially in their specific behavioral expressions. By observing social conventions, youngsters will learn by trial and error to negotiate social occasions. They also need to learn how to make a statement of their individuality by improvising on the scripts that society considers acceptable. Such a balancing act is not easy to pull off; it requires rehearsal, trial-and-error learning, and careful coaching. Too often, in their impatience to complete the lesson, teachers simply encourage a mindless acceptance of social convention.

The Intellectual Version

The intellectual version of the plot of personal formation has teachers sticking to the first business of schools as the training of the mind and exposure to culture. In this view, the best way to encourage personal development is through a rigorous involvement with the classics; the great ideas and ideals of the human spirit; and the discipline of careful expression, debate, and intellectual research. Teachers have enough to do without trying to be a parent or a friend to youngsters. Graduates emerge from the school knowing what is expected of them, and teachers are not to be held accountable for what youngsters do with this knowledge.

This rendition of the plot contains Platonic overtones, namely, that knowledge is equated with virtue, or that knowledge of the principles of virtue compels one to follow the principles of virtue. Critics of this rendition are quick to point out that in fact virtue is acquired through *action* not through knowledge of moral principles. This is not to say that knowledge of moral principles cannot inform action. But virtue is more a matter of action than of understanding. One develops as a person by making choices, putting those choices into action, and then experiencing the consequences of those choices and activities. The consequences do not make the choices right or wrong but do teach the youngster what virtue involves, what it means, and what it feels like. Youngsters have a chance to look at themselves reflexively as they experienced their action, judging whether they liked themselves in the choices they made, judging the impact of those choices on others, and judging whether they would change their actions in similar future situations.

The Accommodation Version

The accommodation plot describes the curriculum of personal formation in terms of the adult responsibilities expected of the students when they leave the school. They are to learn to be productive workers, enabling the nation to be competitive in international markets. They are to be law abiding and responsible citizens. They are expected to be good parents and homemakers. Hence, much of the subject matter of personal formation is geared toward forming the adult qualities required by society. This version of the drama of personal formation suffers from the same limitations as the social contract rendition. It restricts the necessary development of a sense of freedom to be oneself and to make a personal choice of one's life work, rather than accept passively what the authorities mandate or suggest. This rendition of the drama of personal formation can also be a formula for rapid obsolescence. For the most part, schools model their curriculum of personal formation on the present adult world. With technologies changing so rapidly and markets and international trends developing in unforeseen ways, schools may be fixing youngsters' perspectives into a mold that will rapidly become dysfunctional. Similarly, an unchallenged bias toward an Anglo-Saxon expression of cultural life would be inappropriate in the formation of young people for a multicultural world.

The Ideological Version

From an ideological perspective, educators committed to the personal formation of their students may be indoctrinating them into a way of life subtly but firmly bound to an ideology of class, gender, and cultural myths. The studies of Cusick (1973), McLaren (1989), and Sullivan (1990), among others, indicate how easily teachers assume that their own class or race or gender perspective defines the way the world is supposed to work. McLaren (1989), for example, showed how the middle-class attitudes of the brothers teaching in a Canadian Catholic junior high school ran counter to the working-class attitudes of their students and had pretty much the opposite effect of what the brothers intended. Similarly, Lesko's study (1988) of a girls' Catholic high school in the United States revealed how the faculty socialized their students into the cultural norms of academic competition and thus unwittingly defeated other important goals of religious formation, such as teaching the value of community.

One of the best protections against ideological influences is diversity—diversity of class, gender, nationality, and culture. This diversity should be encouraged on the school staff as well as in the student body. The more uniform the staff and the student body, the easier it is for youngsters to acquire the impression that that uniformity defines the way the world is meant to be. Thus an ideology of class, gender, race, and religion creeps in and defines as inferior anyone who is not "like us." In such a school, personal formation takes on a compulsion to embrace the ideology and punish deviance. In a school with lots of diversity among the students and staff, it is easier for a student to be himself or herself. Where everyone is different, it is easier to be different. Questions of what common standards will be required of all may be more difficult to negotiate, but the experience will better prepare youngsters for life in a pluralistic and multicultural world.

The Reproduction Version

The reproduction plot resembles the other versions described above but goes beyond them to emphasize in a self-conscious way (rather than a tacit way) that schools are to enable and encourage the reproduction of society in its present forms. This rendition of the plot places an explicit, primary value on preserving tradition: The tradition represents the collective wisdom of the past and should therefore be honored in its observance and perpetuation. Normally, this is expressed through a classical curriculum; authority relationships; and the perpetuation of social formalities that have governed school life for decades, if not centuries. Exposure to the classics and to the tried-and-true social customs, according to this version, is the best preparation for a youngster to cope with and meet the challenges of adult life. It is also society's way of preserving its civilized way of life and protecting itself from the chaos of fads and fashion, change for the sake of change, and the vulgar elements of mass culture.

This version of the plot of personal formation elevates a healthy concern to preserve cherished traditions into the enthronement of tradition as a dogma that must be memorized and practiced irrespective of the existential demands of particular historical contexts. This plot involves a failure to understand that tradition itself is something that evolved through historical circumstances, whose value and beauty preserve the welfare of the human community by adapting to emerging historical circumstances. From the perspective of the present, tradition's ability to adapt may be concealed by the apparent slowness of that adaptation process, which may give the appearance of timelessness. Tradition was not given from the beginning. It evolved, often through intense periods of high culture. Yet if tradition is to have vitality, it must be seen as the adapting core of a living culture, not a static text that remains unchanged.

A Deeper Look

Most of us would acknowledge that personal formation means more than these one-dimensional plots. A deeper look reveals a much more complex reality, one for which it is difficult to write a plot. We realize that personal formation is not something entered into automatically and from a one-sided framework. It has to be negotiated, agreed upon, and accepted by both students and teachers. That gets us closer to the essence of personal formation. It is relational, always relational. It can never be an isolated, individual exercise; it is necessarily social. Because it is both individual and social, it involves tension and struggle.

The struggle in personal formation is a lifelong struggle over power and meaning. Society, the culture, and other people, even with the best of intentions, try to control our drama. They try to write the script for us. Through punishment, persuasion, reward, and subtle and overt pressures, they try to get us to say our lines correctly. But the lines are not ours. Someone else has written them for us. Hence, we experience the power of others to influence us to perform according to their definitions. Yet each of us has the unique power—which no one can take from us—to be ourselves. No one else has the power to be me. Only I have it. But it is not an absolute power. We cannot be ourselves in isolation from the culture, in isolation from language and dialect, in isolation from convention and tradition. These both enable and constrain. They set artificial boundaries, channel action in certain directions, and encourage unreflective routine. They also give us the tools of expression by which we can make ourselves understood by others, the symbolic systems whereby we can express externally our inner self (Bowers, 1987; Shils, 1981).

Youngsters who drop out of school or who continually create problems in school are often saying through their actions, "I refuse you the power to define my drama, to package my life for me. *I* will define my place in the social drama, not you." One of the subtle but real experiences of youngsters when they come to school is that of powerlessness. They are turned over, as it were, into the hands of a group of adults who can control every minute of the school day. Youngsters are rarely if ever asked what they want to do in school. They are told what to do and punished if they fail to do it. Moreover, school authorities have the power to call the youngster's parents on the carpet to give them a dressing down for the uncooperative behavior of their child. Imagine how powerful school authorities must appear to children, when their parents—the most powerful people in the child's life—can be threatened and be made to feel ashamed by school staff.

In the personal formation of youngsters in school, educators are supposed to help youngsters grow in their power to be themselves while at the same time helping them come to terms with the legitimate exercise of power by the community to protect and safeguard the social drama. In helping youngsters to develop their power to be themselves, educators enter with them into the mystery and paradox of human relationships. Only when we let someone else be themselves can we truly love them; only when we let someone love us and know us as we are can we become ourselves. The power to be ourselves is enriched and fully exercised in relationship. That is what school should be teaching youngsters.

The plot of personal formation also involves youngsters in a lifelong struggle for meaning. One can only understand one's own meaning by understanding the meaning of the social drama. Who is to define the meaning of the social drama? Is the meaning of the social drama the survival of the fittest? a struggle of the disenfranchised for emancipation? a journey into isolated self-discovery? a journey of God's children into the Promised Land? a perpetual reenactment of the cycles of nature?

In schools, educators are supposed to help youngsters explore a variety of explanations of the social drama and what those explanations imply for their personal life. The study of history is supposed to help youngsters interpret their collective present. Study of science is supposed to help youngsters understand how nature works, how humans are to be stewards of nature, how the rhythms and patterns of nature are reflected in their bodies and minds. Study of literature is supposed to help youngsters recognize their struggles in the struggles of the characters in the story. Again, youngsters who drop out of or indifferently drift through school are often saying indirectly that they do not like or accept what *we* say the social drama means. The worst crime is committed by students who never question what the authorities tell them the drama means.

The underlying plot of personal formation is the pursuit and discovery of those basic meanings that ground our lives as persons and as communities. That search and discovery is never ending; it is always incomplete. We continually discover new meanings or new depths to familiar meanings. The crucial point of this search is the insight that meanings that support my own sense of worth, dignity, and heroic destiny are also the meanings that support the value and heroic destiny of the community. The meaning of the social drama should not pit the individual against society. The point of personal formation is to discover and create those large meanings of the drama that make it work both for the community and for the individuals within it.

In any given school, educators need to examine how their present practice of personal formation enables youngsters to find themselves and to be themselves in the very process of creating and sustaining a vibrant, joyous, and caring community. Is the present process of personal formation presenting youngsters with a script written by the chamber of commerce or an obsolete Eurocentric cultural elite? Is the social drama of school life a living drama in which genuine characters play their parts and, while learning the available language, costuming, gestures, and conventions of the play, use these to express and create themselves?

Forming a Character

My version of the plot of the drama of personal formation has the teacher encouraging the youngster to be an authentic character in the social drama. That is to say, along with parents and other significant persons in the youngster's life, the teacher helps to form a distinct human person who knows how to act and to find meaning within the social drama (Starratt, 1990). Personal formation means attempting to equip youngsters with the necessary conventions and understandings of the social drama while at the same time encouraging them to discover who they want to be.

This plot of personal formation is intended to get the youngster to understand the larger social plot as a human construct, made by humans for the benefit of humans. It is a plot whose script is imperfect, always needing improvement in order to make the human drama work better for people. Personal formation, then, means helping youngsters to become more intentionally involved with their creation of themselves as a character, both through learning the social scripts and through learning how to improvise on them for their own benefit and the benefit of their fellows. Being a character in the drama means understanding others in the drama and being able to enter into authentic relationships with the other characters in the play. Personal formation always and ultimately involves forming community.

It is important to insist on the social nature of personal formation. All persons by themselves are incomplete. We become complete in activity with others. Our spirit engages with another spirit and in so doing we become more than we are as an isolated being. Youngsters form themselves by continuing to explore their world, the world of strangers and friends, the world of ideas and meanings, the world of experience. In reaching out and making contact with their world, they are finding out what they like and dislike about themselves, what others like or dislike about them, what they can or cannot do well. The journey is not simply the journey of the individual—it is a journey of the individual's generation, of the peers, and, ultimately, of the whole community. What any given youngster becomes affects others. What the community is and is becoming affects the individual's becoming.

The Players

Again, we can identify superficial definitions of the players in this dramaturgy. The adult knows the script, youth does not. The adult is virtuous, youth is impulsive. The adult is mature, youth is immature. Too often we conceive adulthood as the achievement of an ever-constant stability, an arrival at the fullness of life; youth are those who have not reached this threshold after which people live happily ever after.

The Developmental Dimension

When we view the players developmentally, we see that both youth and adults are involved in the same process, namely, of moving through stages of life. Both adults and youngsters are involved in dynamics of growth, although the stages of life they are growing through and into are different. Growing involves struggle, fear, successes, and failures for all players. Think of two extremes. In the best of circumstances, the teacher has successfully negotiated the stage of childhood (and consequently has a basic trust of others and of life) and the stage of adolescence (and consequently has a stable sense of identity). At the other extreme, the teacher may have failed to negotiate those stages of development. Nonetheless he or she is expected to assist, nay, *form* young people who are negotiating their stage of development. Between these extreme cases, we find ourselves—we have moved through the stages of life more or less successfully but occasionally find the residue of unresolved issues still causing us trouble.

Young people are *not* adults. Often, we adults tell them, "Grow up!"—in other words, we expect them to act as adults. But youth need the time and space to be young, to play, to fantasize, to explore the world. We should all go back to read Rousseau's *Emile* every 5 years or so to be reminded to let children be children and learn the way children learn, with all the false starts and meanderings and delight of discovery. Some schools proceed as though learning requires youngsters to be passive, as teachers pour gallons of knowledge and advice into their supposedly empty heads. In such ways, schools treat children as clients, rather than as players in a drama.

The Moral Dimension

A closer look at the players in a moral framework is revealing. We feel free to correct young people, to admonish them for their faults and blunders. We know that youngsters need advice and careful monitoring. We hope that they will internalize the advice and learn how to monitor and correct themselves. But what about us? Are we not a mix of human failings and human virtues? Do we not in our everyday lives find self-serving motives and rationalizations constantly intruding upon our thoughts, conversations, and actions?

The players in the dramaturgy of personal formation are both fragile and filled with potential. We human beings carry around fears and anxieties, yearnings and frustrations, dreams and nightmares. At one time or another, we face threats of injury and death, humiliation and ridicule, inconsequentiality and failure. Sometimes, threatening experiences, frustrating experiences, or simple boredom lead us to do some wacky, crazy, or even horrible things. Humans also do wonderful things: Mothers make extraordinary sacrifices for their children; friends exhibit loyalty under the most trying circumstances; people tell the truth when lying would gain them a fortune.

In the dramaturgy of personal formation, we need to see both educators and youngsters as complex, flawed, and wonderful human beings. Both sets of players are capable of stupid, cruel, and deceitful behavior and they are also capable of intelligent, generous, and loyal behavior. We sometimes fail to realize that children see our weaknesses as much as we see theirs. When we admonish them as though we are without fault, they may be learning a different lesson than we intend, the lesson of hypocrisy. Before assuming the responsibility of forming a young person, we need to take stock of ourselves, of our need for forgiveness and compassion. Perhaps, what we have most to offer in the personal formation process is an understanding of what the struggle for personal integrity entails. It may be very important to admit to our students that we sometimes do not understand ourselves and our motives. They need to know that we, too, experience relationships that do not work well all the time.

Personal Formation in Community

I believe we have to reconceive personal formation in the schools, not as taking place between two people—one who possesses technical skills in personal formation that she or he administers to a client and another who simply learns by listening—but rather as a process constantly engaging both parties as members of a community. Personal formation happens in the daily interaction between people. We form ourselves by the way we *all* act—that is, the community is a kind of collective super teacher. Cumulatively, all teach all. The way we conduct our relationships forms us, and by the example we give to one another, we are part of the community helping to form others, some of whom we do not know. This is what Aristotle was getting at in his treatises on ethics and politics, namely that it is the polis, the civic community, that educates morally (Sullivan, 1986). It does this in the everyday interaction of people dealing with the practical affairs of their lives. In these transactions, stories are told, traditions recalled, and rituals enacted that tacitly reveal obligations and relationships (Jackson, Boostrom, & Hansen, 1993).

Within this large environment of personal formation, there is room for one-on-one interaction. Educators need to have a relationship with each youngster. They have to care about her or him and enjoy doing some things with her or him. It is in the relationship that life is shared and exchanged and nurtured. Insofar as formation actually takes place—and by formation I mean the internalizing of an experience so that it becomes tacitly normative—it takes place in the give-and-take of two people who communicate with each other out of a sense of positive regard. If the adult is simply an authority figure, a police officer, a judge, then most healthy youngsters set up barriers and strategies to defend themselves from the adult's attacks on their person. They will not let you inside; they won't let you touch them, even though you bash them around a bit. It is only when we deal with the inside of youngsters that lasting effects of a relationship take root.

In speaking about an ideal teacher-student relationship, William Arrowsmith (1985) argues that the teacher has to interpret and impersonate a deep sense of humanity, which undergirds the whole curriculum. Youngsters often naively think that teachers know all there is to know on a given topic. The student believes that the teacher of Shakespeare knows every play backward and forward and can uncover all the difficult and multiple meanings behind every line. The science teacher knows all the mysteries of biology or physics and represents the collective wisdom of all the scientists who ever were. The teacher of mathematics is Archimedes, Descartes, Plank, and Einstein all wrapped in one. The students' expectations of their teachers tend to draw out the best in the teachers. On any given day, the teacher does represent and "impersonate" the collective intelligence of the human race in a given area. Students' expectations compel teachers to stand on tiptoes toward the texts being taught and the humanity they embody, to become that humanity for the student. Hence, it becomes more apparent that the teacher-student relationship in personal formation affects the teacher as well, drawing out the best in the teacher.

As educators, we ought to know these things. We ought to see the connection between giving life, giving love, and the personal formation of the young. Showing all children positive regard and telling them that they are special provides them the space to believe in themselves and make choices to share their lives with others. Virtue is not what youngsters learn from us so much as it is their choosing to be virtuous. Our formation of them in a life of virtue is much more a matter of us loving them enough so that they can choose to be virtuous. All the things we teach youngsters that make up the curriculum of personal formation take place naturally in conversations between two people who care about one another. And this best takes place when the youngster comes to the teacher with a question, rather than when the teacher, with an anthology of all the answers to life's questions, constantly hovers over the child.

Does this mean that we should never correct youngsters? By no means. But it does mean that we correct them from within a relationship of caring. Does that mean the youngsters will never violate that relationship? No. But we should always remember the lesson about removing the log from our own eye before attempting to remove the sawdust from the eye of someone else. Recognizing that we ourselves have failed and continue to fail in relationships, we need to adopt the role of the wounded healer. When we correct youngsters, it must be in the way we would want to be corrected—with gentleness and respect; leaving the person intact; and communicating a sense of compassionate understanding, even while showing how the behavior causes problems in the person's relationships. If we must be critics, let us be loving critics for whom the relationship is more important than the scoring of critical points.

The Community Dimension

The stress on the relational character of personal formation leads us to another important realization about that drama. The teachers are not the primary influence in personal formation within the school. The students are. Numerous studies of school effects have indicated that the impact of the student body on the achievement and attitudes of students is next to that of the home environment and more influential than specific school programs or interactions with teachers. Studies of cooperative learning, for example, indicate greater learning gains through working with peers than working under the direction of a teacher. A study of the effects of community service programs indicates that diversity within the student body, more than the programs themselves, had a greater correlation with the development of empathy among the students. Most of Kohlberg's (1981a) research on moral development favors placing youngsters in groups of students of diverse stages of development to maximize the cognitive moral development of participants. All these studies indicate the strong influence of other students on personal formation.

It follows from this that the school can have a large influence on personal formation by creating an environment in the school that promotes peer interaction. Some schools have initiated peer counseling groups, peer tutoring groups, student-led conflict resolution teams, student-led retreats, student-designed liturgies. Other schools are exploring a much larger role for student government within the school. The point seems to be to maximize the good influence youngsters can have on one another.

The Possibilities

When we think of personal formation in terms of the drama, we see that the outcomes of this kind of education are fraught with weighty consequences. The feeling of drama precisely derives from not knowing how things will turn out, yet knowing how a fatal move can have lifelong consequences. We can perhaps direct our improvisations of this drama by imagining those possibilities that structure the drama toward a happy conclusion for the players involved. Let me offer abbreviated, idealized script for a school seeking to enhance its personal formation of students.

In this script, the drama of personal formation would be the enterprise of a community of educators who value the diversity on the staff as a source of enrichment to their own lives. This would be a community of adults who themselves are growing through life stages, who are willing to talk about the joys and pains of such growth experiences, who are comfortable acknowledging that they still have miles to grow before they can rest. These are also adults who are in touch with what is going on in the world outside the school, not simply in the area of sport, but in the fields of politics, economics, the arts, and sciences. Obviously, most will not be experts in all areas. Collectively, however, they are able to engage the youngsters in discussions of the exciting happenings and challenges in their world.

This staff would create in the school a graduated series of experiences that engage the students in groups of various sizes and composition (same level, mixed levels). These experiences would be built to nurture those human qualities the staff particularly valued and wanted *each* youngster to be exposed to. There would be some effort at a common personal formation. These experiences could be organized around themes or dialectics, such as experiences emphasizing being over having, living over achieving, communication over entertainment, owing over owning, public participation over private self-indulgence.

These experiences could also be designed around the topic of self-discovery: in tradition, in nature, in relationships, in creative action. Because self-discovery is such an individual process, the experiences could be open to a host of possibilities. These experiences could have papers or projects attached to them, or simply conclude with some lively discussions and reflection.

Besides these common experiences in personal formation, the staff would have initiated a yearly sequence of discussions and reflections on the quality of life in the school (Oliver, 1976). The idea behind this would be to encourage the youngsters to take responsibility for the quality of their communal life. If there is bullying and scapegoating going on, how do they propose to stop it? If they feel the school spirit declining, how do they propose to bolster it? The school community would become a source for personal formation as the youngsters attempted to improve the practical carrying out of their daily tasks. Special project teams and standing committees of the student government could be assigned to oversee the resolutions passed by the student body concerning their common life in the school.

When the school community is sufficiently organized to handle the common issues that students feel support a quality common life, there will still be individual personal formation needs. Individual teacher-student relationships will allow for conversations to take place where uncertainties can be resolved, questions posed, problems analyzed. Again, the practical working through of problems will usually be the vehicle for the ongoing formation of youngsters.

Summing Up

Early on in the discussion of leadership in this book, it should have become clear that leadership is not carried out by Lone Rangers. Leadership is effective insofar as the leader can attract and nurture the leadership of others in the organization. All too often in discussions about school leadership, this means developing the leadership of teachers; seldom are the students mentioned in this context. I suggest here that the leadership of the principal will be most effective when it activates the leadership of all the stakeholders, including the students. The vision of schooling that has at its heart the personal formation of the students' lives by the students themselves necessarily calls forth leadership qualities in all the students. Their full participation in the work of the school is what will make the school ultimately successful. The job of the principal is to invite everyone to participate in this drama.

⪻ 8 ⪼

The Politics of
Reform and the Life World

As we puzzle over the very complex realities of schooling in the United States and the reform or restructuring efforts taking place there, we may feel overwhelmed by the attempt to make sense of it. Addressing the problems of schooling in the United States involves addressing the problems of the nation. The nation is "at risk," as one of the early national reports of the 1980s put it (National Commission on Excellence in Education, 1983), but what is at risk is, I fear, much more than what the authors of that document conceived. As a professor involved in graduate programs designed to stimulate and nurture the leadership of educational administrators, I struggle with my students to understand the underlying issues and agendas that drive the reform movement, so that we can explore authentic leadership responses to, and our potential shaping of, the forces involved.

At the outset, then, I seek to establish a more basic understanding of the predicament we educators find ourselves in. With that frame-

work of understanding, we can develop more particular analyses of
leadership and school renewal.

The Life World

One way I can make sense out of what is happening in the United
States is to employ a distinction I came across in the works of Jurgen
Habermas (1970, 1971) and Anthony Giddens (1984). It is the distinction between what they call the *life world* and the world of mass administration and mass production. The life world is the world of
natural human relationships, the face-to-face life of people within
family and extended family, the world of intimacy and friendship. In
native societies (often patronizingly labeled "primitive") the life
world encompasses everything: the child's birth in the home, the
raising and socialization of children, education in the myths and traditions and history of the community, rites of passage at various
stages of life, religious rituals, work and commerce, and immersion
in the rhythms of nature and the seasons.

The World of
Mass Administration and Production

With the coming of modernity, especially in the 19th and 20th
centuries, we find another kind of world emerging—a more artificial
world of the state and of commerce. Public life becomes fragmented,
compartmentalized, and rationalized through the public administration of the state. The state regulates banking and education, food
production and the use of airwaves, travel and commerce, law courts
and the dumping of garbage. Commerce is separated from the home.
Workers work in factories and firms where work is governed by goals
of efficiency and maximization of productivity, not by kinship rela-
tions or the rhythms of nature and the seasons.

The artificial world of mass production and mass administration
gradually, but relentlessly, has intruded more and more on the life
world of family and neighborhood. The government increasingly
regulates the life world through laws that govern marriage and

divorce, the sending of children to compulsory schooling, the availability of health care, the construction of homes and public housing, the setting aside and use of retirement incomes. The commercial world commodifies more and more of the life world, replacing family agriculture with the supermarket; herbal healing with commercial drugs; the village square as the hub for news and gossip with newspapers, society columns, talk shows, and TV news. Even romance is commodified through dating services, wedding consultants, honeymoon packages, and, subsequently, marriage counseling. One of the more offensive intrusions of the commercial world on the life world is the greeting card, with boilerplate statements of affection for Valentine's Day and birthdays, and worse, mass-produced religious sentiments in cards for religious holidays. Television has replaced the family and neighborhood storytellers. Family life, especially in the evening, is organized around TV shows and news programs purporting to tell the audience what's new, what's happening in the world—all the while interspersing the flow of action with commercials selling still more commodities.

Colonization of the Life World

The life world is where we learn to be human; the continuous experience of family intimacy and neighborhood relationships is the natural seedbed of human affections and values and selfhood. The life world is the network of face-to-face relationships in which human beings engage in both trivial and serious conversations, negotiate conflicts, express how they feel about aspects of their lives. It is where people laugh and joke with each other and commiserate over common sufferings. In the life world, people make things for one another such as clothing, meals, and toys for the children. There people experience nature firsthand through planting and watering and weeding and harvesting. Youngsters see birth and death, sickness and recovery as natural events. In the life world, people experience tragedy, pain, and loss, as well as the joys of intimacy, the satisfactions of friendships, and the loyalties of family. There they sing and dance to celebrate days of remembrance and days of sacred events.

This life world, however, has been increasingly "colonized," as Habermas (1975) has said, by the artificial world of mass administration and production. This is a world of rational order, of the manipulation of desire and fantasy through advertising. This world reduces individuality to predictable uniformity in state policy formation; it quantifies interpersonal relationships and work and leisure into cost-benefit formulae and long-range plans. The mind-set of this artificial world affects the private citizen and the business executive, as well as the public official. Living and working exclusively within this mind-set dehumanizes us all.

Yet educators are urged to incorporate this mind-set as they set about the work of reforming the schools. It is common to hear recommendations that schools be managed according to "accepted business procedures." I confess to a certain ambivalence about these recommendations. We hear almost daily reports that one or another corporate executive, real estate agent, investment banker, or government official has colluded in monopolizing a market, denuding the environment, savaging urban populations, and defrauding clients while skirting the sanctions of the law and lining their pockets. I tend to be skeptical of the sanctimonious demands of the corporate world that education be held accountable to the public. Where did such a sanitized and righteous view of big business come from?

This is not to say that the life world is all sweetness and light. It is also the world of jealousies and hatred, of parental violence against children, of madness and cruelty. That part of the life world deserves public regulation and therapeutic attention. But we educators should remind ourselves when considering the proposals of the state and commercial worlds that their worlds are also affected by greed, lust for power, self-serving rationalization, and not just a little insanity.

The colonization of the life world by the artificial world of mass administration and mass commodity production and consumption has clearly affected all aspects of schools. Students experience being treated as things—intellects expected to absorb required information and then to repeat it, untouched by their own sentiments and experiences, on exams. Achievement in school means meeting uniform standards set for everyone more often than a personal response to the curriculum.

The bureaucratic administration of school systems shapes the administration of individual schools. Students are to be controlled. Prepackaged curriculum is "delivered" to them. Uniform learnings are expected from uniform "treatments." Students' sexuality and cultural differences are an embarrassment to the statistical assessment of learning. Their physical energy is constantly distracting the teacher from her or his lesson plan. Their rebellion against rules they had no say in formulating is to be smothered at all cost. In some schools, it appears that students are the adversary. In many classrooms, students hear the unspoken message: "No thinking for yourself, thank you. We don't need your uniqueness or your cultural difference or your creativity, only your conformity to our agenda."

Separation of the Life World of Children From That of Adults

With the erosion of the family unit and the accompanying increase of homes where both parents work, preschoolers go to day care centers, and schoolchildren return to empty houses, what Coleman and Hoffer (1987) called the "social capital" that children bring to school is diminished. Children's reference group for social learning is their peer group. Many children have not sufficiently experienced the consistent, caring relationship with adults that forms the basis of learning to be *social* beings. With the impoverishment of their family life, their grounding in common values and meanings of the adult community is eroded. Their life world is limited mostly to interactions with other children whose social capital is similarly attenuated. Child recreation, games, drinking, surfing, MTV, contests for the most outlandish or hip forms of costume and coiffure, code language, "hanging out"—these characterize the life world of young people. This is not to say that among themselves they do not occasionally develop standards of heroism or trust. Nevertheless, those standards are often deviant from and outside of the influence of the adult community. Underneath their experienced life world is a feeling of alienation from the world of adults, whether that involves the arena of work, schooling, or civic responsibility. The lives of children have been trivialized. Devoid of deep, caring relationships with adults, empty of any challenge to make a contribution to the life of their familial or civil community, confronted in school with learning tasks that appear to have little connection with anything real, their life world with their peers offers them the only place to go. But that place offers little sense, value, or meaning other than entertainment and recreation and a status defined within the narrow confines of the group. Having fun comes to define their horizon.

What results from all this? A massive alienation of young people from schooling. Deep down they recognize the trivialization of learning. Academic studies have less and less contact with their life world. Their hopes and fears, their longings and uncertainties are not addressed. Instead, their schooling experiences are managed, controlled, commodified, and artificialized by those in authority.

School leadership in this artificial world of mass administration and mass production is understood as management of inputs and outputs, efficient delivery of services, and productivity measured by test scores. You see, it makes perfect sense for officials of government and industry to colonize the schools, demanding that schools serve national economic policies. In their minds, schools exist to further the interests of the state and of commercial enterprise, for that is what defines, for them, public life. Hence, school administration is expected to mirror government and business administration. The world of school can be reduced to predictable, controllable, uniform elements of policy implementation. The state and commercial administrators define what skills are required and the schools promptly turn out compliant workers with the required skills.

Imagining Other Possibilities

Another possibility, of course, is that educators exert another kind of leadership, a leadership that connects the world of teaching and learning with the life world of the community. I am not suggesting that it is possible to return to the organic community of the "primitive" life world. The world of state government and commercial enterprise is a world that is here to stay. But it does not have to be a world that smothers and destroys the life world. The two worlds do not have to be so antithetical to each other. They can, as a matter of fact, enhance the values of each other. Such an integration requires a profound transformation of worldviews. I believe that this is precisely the challenge facing educators today: to participate in a national effort to create an ongoing dialogue between both worlds. This is the social agenda of transforming institutional life so that it honors human meanings and values at the same time as it addresses 21st-century challenges.

Educational leaders with this kind of vision will respond to the demands of the state and of industry with an emerging vision of schooling that grounds school learning in the larger life world of the community—a vision that challenges youngsters to work, even while in school, to understand both the possibilities and the dangers of living in a mass-administered society and a world of mass production and consumption. The dangers are acute for those whose life world is severed from concern for moral striving, personal responsibility, responsibility to the environment, and the human quest for both freedom and community. This kind of educational leadership sees the curriculum of the school consisting precisely in the work of uniting the two worlds in a creative tension, allowing neither the artificial world to dominate the human agenda, nor the humanistic agenda to ignore the demands of nation building and economic productivity.

Curriculum Implications

Principals and teachers can easily examine the present curriculum to see where links can be established between the youngster's life world and their school learning. There are any number of connections between the science they study and technological applications in the home, from electricity, heating systems, water pressure, and automobiles to home gardens, food preservatives, medicines, television, and so on. In history classes, teachers can use local oral histories from grandparents and neighbors and the archives of local organizations such as churches and synagogues, the chamber of commerce, the Red Cross, the NAACP, the zoning commission, and so on. In language arts, children can write their own short stories and poetry. Much of this is already done by good teachers.

Schools can raise issues of where the rationality of mass production comes into conflict with human values, such as in the case of manufacturers who cut corners on consumer safety guidelines to cut costs and maximize profits, financial companies who foreclose on family farms that have been continued for four or five generations, and employers who fire workers 6 months from retirement. Schools can raise questions over whether there might have been ways that the businesses involved might have handled things differently so that the impact on human lives could have been softened, or indeed, whether the people involved could have benefited by a different course of action.

Even as schools teach respect for those in authority, they can also teach youngsters what legal means are available to them when it appears that there has been an abuse of authority or negligence by those in authority. Schools can teach the lesson that one's work or career is a way of serving other people, a way of making a contribution to the well-being of the community. Schools need to play their part in preparing a workforce that is not only technologically smarter but morally more responsible to the public interest. Schools also need to teach that political office brings with it the highest moral responsibility to make democracy work. This lesson can be taught not only in social studies classes, but through the student government in the school and through the daily lessons in self-governance in the corridors, playground, and cafeteria.

Schools need to teach youngsters that wealth is not simply a matter of money in the bank or owning lots of things. Youngsters need to learn that health, both physical and mental, is wealth; that friends and family are wealth. Schools can teach the necessary lesson that clean air and water is the community's wealth, as is peace among communities and peoples. Diversity is wealth. Time is wealth. Experience of the sacred enriches human life. Volunteer community resources are wealth. All these elements of the human enterprise constitute wealth in their own right. Such messages help to counterbalance the overemphasis on money and possessions. We have had too many youngsters lose their lives over a leather jacket or a new pair of sneakers.

Links With Other Protectors of the Life World

The challenge to create a healthy balance between the demands of the life world and the demands of a mass-administered, mass-producing and mass-consuming social order will remain on the social and political agenda for our society for a long time to come. Educators need to forge links with other groups with a stake in creating and preserving this balance. They can provide ideas and resources and political leverage. Beyond the need for a national conversation among educators, invitations to other groups need to be extended. Besides business and government people, other voices will be important to hear. The voices of women are important, for they have consistently championed the values of the life world: the values of family life, care for children, better health care for people, more humane working conditions, the primacy of relationships. Another important voice is the voice of the church educator who has struggled to develop a language and a learning environment that honors the sense of the sacred and a sense for moral integrity and community building while continuing to educate for a pluralistic, secular public life. Other voices to be heard are those of native peoples whose life world is so strongly rooted in a feeling for the land and the mysteries of nature. The voices of artists are likewise important, for they lead us beneath the surface of life to confront the terrible beauty of human and natural life. By including these and other voices in the national conversation, educators will be able to forge a vision of schooling that brings the two worlds closer together—never, perhaps, in perfect harmony, but at least in a healthier, more creative tension.

Summing Up

In the United States, educators are being asked to reduce education to simplistic formulae to fit into a commodified and administered world. But such a reduction of education is self-defeating. The United States will become a great nation not because its schools produce efficient workers, but because the schools grow great people, people who find their life world fulfilled in their public life and work and politics, people who transform public life into an arena of moral striving and human fulfillment.

₠ 9 ₢

The Moral Leadership
of School Reform

The announcement of policies of school reform by state authorities sometimes carries overtones of an authoritarian order being imposed on people who have made a mess of things in the past who are now being called to account and told how to behave in the future. At the same time, the policies and their guidelines are worded in the language of technical management: efficiency, accountability, measurement of outcomes, carefully rationalized and articulated sequences of activities and procedures, and monitoring and reporting systems to ensure compliance. This style of promulgating reform policies seems to assume a similar style of administrative response throughout the educational system, namely an authoritarian, technical management style. In this final chapter, I want to suggest that major educational reform requires a fundamentally different approach and response, one that situates the demanding technical work of reform within a moral perspective of human social life that the reforms are meant to serve.

Moral Leadership

The present reform efforts require a moral response from educators, a response described in the language of leadership. The magnitude of the social consequences implied in present reform policies requires not simply an administrative response, but beyond that, a leadership response (Greenfield, 1995). School reform will not come about through a uniform application of policy. Rather, school reform requires an interpretation of policy in the light of local circumstances and an implementation of policy that encourages local understanding of the meanings and values behind the policies—a blending of the new initiatives with the talent and strengths and resources locally available, and with a realistic assessment of the local obstacles to carrying out the policy. Rather than a mindless obedience to "the authorities"—whoever they may be—the response to the call for school reform requires the moral leadership of school administrators.

Learning From Studies of Policy Implementation

When confronted by a call for large, sweeping reform in education, a leader will ask, "What has been our experience with attempts at large, sweeping reforms in the past?" The literature is instructive. Evaluation studies of attempted major changes in U.S. schools have shown the schools to be remarkably resourceful in absorbing innovations and neutralizing their impact (Popkewitz, 1979; Sarason, 1982). Policy studies reveal a similar pattern (Boyd, 1987). Policies made at a distance from those who must implement them and from those who must live with them rarely achieve the objectives of the policy. Decisions from the top are blunted at every level in the chain of command by people who want, for a variety of reasons, to maintain the status quo. By contrast, those policies that make it through to implementation so that they effect what the policy actually intended are those that engaged the participants early on in discussions about the purposes of the policy, the integration of that policy into existing operations, and the procedures for implementing the policy (Berman & McLaughlin, 1977; Huberman & Miles, 1983).

Social change does not occur automatically, nor easily. On the contrary, social change, up until recent history, tended to be the exception rather than the rule. On the individual, small group, and societal levels, there is an enormous drag toward stasis, or equilibrium. People want the familiar routine, the predictable patterns. Order, security, peace of mind, cognitive consistency—these enable us to get through the day as individuals and societies. On the individual level, we distort evidence right in front of us to maintain our chosen attitudes and beliefs:

> The organization of knowledge in the mind is like a library system; our built-in biases allow us to retrieve any specific information that we need rapidly; once we make a commitment to a particular cataloguing system (say, a conservative ideology or a religious framework of belief), we spend more time maintaining the system than revising it. (Tavris, 1982, p. 229)

Social mores and traditions provide a constant, though usually subliminal, understanding of the "way things are" (and are supposed to be) (Shils, 1981). When new policies threaten the routine and the predictable, individuals and groups react and resist, not necessarily out of malice, bad judgment, or laziness, but more often because the change requires an unaccustomed shift in familiar procedures, relationships, definitions, or patterns that have come to define reality itself.

Often, the appearance of change is in fact merely a series of readjustments, as a system absorbs small variations in its basic pattern and maintains its own pace and direction (Burns, 1978). The decisions of policymakers cause a slight alteration and then the social system restores its equilibrium.

Although the situation is still quite fluid, we seem to be witnessing a more concerted, enduring effort at major, systemwide change in education. National and state officials have been devoting considerable time and political action to the reform of schools for at least a decade, and there appears no slackening on the horizon. As a result, school restructuring has affected school district and school-based administrators. However, their posture tends toward passive acceptance of directives from above, rather than a leadership response of

probing the values and assumptions behind the reform efforts, pointing to unanticipated consequences to the changes, and suggesting
adaptations of the policy that may counterbalance a tendency toward
one-dimensional views of education. Such a leadership response is
called for because as McNeil (1988) has shown in her research, the
very control mechanisms that policymakers put in place to ensure
identifiable improvement in learning have ended up trivializing the
educational process with results quite opposite to those intended.
What is needed is administrative leadership throughout the system, so that adequate discussion of policy initiatives can take place
up and down the chain of command before the policy is promulgated
(Starratt, 1988).

Leadership of the Principal

Leadership at all levels is called for to carry out a large-scale
reform of the nation's school system, but leadership at the school
level is especially necessary (Goodlad, 1984). Although their leadership will be shaped by district guidelines, the school principals know
that the school is the real locus of change. The scale of their leadership
involves manageable arenas of action; it involves adequate contact
with those affected by changes so that they feel a part of the decision
to initiate and implement them. The school leader enjoys sufficient
access to the school community to engage it in the value questions
embedded in school renewal. The leader and followers are engaged
at a level that still allows for moral agency. We begin to understand
how critical local principals will be for the implementation of state
reform policies.

Given the pluralistic nature of modern societies, regional and
local leaders will need to consult a variety of groups in the community. As people debate the costs and benefits of a particular policy,
they help to clarify and redefine the issues. Problems and issues are
renamed and alternative solutions more thoroughly explored. Hold-
ers of conflicting interests argue for their point of view. Debate will
grow heated and unruly, but that is often the only way to get the
issues on the table for public discussion and out of the back room

where special interest deals are made at the expense of the majority. Conflict is therefore a good to be valued, rather than a nuisance to be avoided. Early consensus, on the contrary, can be deceptive; it usually masks a process of setting policy by excluding discussions with those most adversely affected by the policy.

Transactional and Transformational Leadership

In considering the moral dimensions of leadership, I find Burns's (1978) categories of transactional and transformational leadership particularly helpful. *Transactional leadership* is concerned with moral values such as honesty, fairness, loyalty, integrity, responsibility. It is that leadership whereby one sees to it that people enter into agreements that arc clear, aboveboard, and take into account the rights and needs of others. It is the leadership of the administrator who sees to the day-to-day management of the system, listening to the complaints and concerns of various participants, arbitrating disputes fairly, holding people accountable to their job targets, providing necessary resources for the achievement of subunit goals, and so on. We may call it leadership rather than management because the activity is raised to a moral level by a commitment to human values. Of itself, management is neither moral or immoral; its primary concern is logic, efficiency, order, predictability, and productivity. One could manage an extermination camp or a monastery. Transactions between human beings are raised to a moral plane when they are governed by principles of honesty, fairness, responsibility, and loyalty, because those values are intrinsic to the pragmatic carrying on of genuinely human life. Transactional leadership deals with persons seeking their own individual, independent objectives. It involves a bargaining between the individual interests of persons or groups in return for their cooperation in the leader's agenda.

Transformational leadership, on the other hand, involves seeking to elevate people's views beyond self-interest to a joint effort on behalf of common aims. Transformational leaders bring people to act on behalf of the collective interests of their group or community. The premise of this leadership is that whatever separate interests or goals individuals might have, they are united with the leader in the pursuit of higher goals.

Transformational leadership, therefore, is concerned with large, collective values such as freedom, equity, community, justice, brotherhood, and sisterhood. It is that leadership that calls people's attention to the basic purpose of the organization and to the relationship between the organization and society. This leadership is an elevating activity that lifts people beyond their routine and pragmatic concerns to a commitment to higher purposes (Vaill, 1984). It is an activity that unites people behind a collective goal that enables them to pool their energies, which can easily get dispersed in seeking individual or subgroup goals. Transforming leadership changes people's operative attitudes, values, and beliefs from self-centered to higher, altruistic beliefs, attitudes, and values.

The implementation of school reform clearly requires transactional leadership of the middle-range type. In the conduct of education we find a number of conflicting claims and demands being made on the schools. Before any major decisions can be made or new policy enacted, numerous "transactions" must take place. The needs and interests of various constituencies must be taken into account. Given limits to funding and other resources such as time and space, the system must be managed as a limited system. Not everyone's claims can be fully accommodated. Whatever solution is negotiated, however, must be carried out according to procedures that are fair to all parties involved, in an atmosphere of respect and honesty, and with measures of accountability that ensure all parties know what is expected of them and others.

In many cases, administrators will be facing new situations and will have to invent new rules for the game. Or the complexity of the problem and the intensity with which positions are held will require streamlining and simplifying procedures to allow for temporary or provisional actions. In all of this, administrators will have to appeal not only to rationality but also to people's moral sensibilities. As Mead (1983) suggests,

> A community can achieve an overall public good only if its various groups observe limits on their own immediate claims. . . . Rational

action for the collectivity depends on non-rational—civic, dutiful, restrained—action by individuals. . . . Only on these moral bases could government restrain self-seeking and eventually achieve a public interest. (p. 168)

Such an appeal to teachers, to teacher unions, and to parents seems appropriate in those instances where an uncompromising demand for what is theirs by contract or by statute causes a disproportionate hardship for others, especially for students. This is not to excuse administrators from attempting in every instance to honor those statutory or contractual agreements. On the other hand, teachers and parents might yield their rights in a particular instance to bring about a larger, collective good. I may not be obligated by any law to come to the aid of a person struck down by an automobile. But a larger, collective good is served when people voluntarily go beyond what the law requires.

To return to our focus on the transactional leadership of the principal, this kind of leadership will be very attentive to those policies and guidelines that influence staffing and promotion patterns, decision making, and conflict-mediating procedures. These transactional leaders will continue to seek improvements in program evaluation, vertical and horizontal communication networks, subunit coordination, specific target-setting strategies, and the work of problem-solving task forces. Their leadership will be guided by technical expertise, rationality, and a sense of the limits of rationality. That will involve getting the facts clear, naming the problem clearly, exploring alternatives, keeping decisions close to the local practitioners, and using their intuitions and common sense. These kinds of leaders will encourage debate and discussion of conflicting points of view, recognizing how important this is for clarifying what the stakes are and encouraging ownership of the final decision. The process of hearing everyone's claims educates others to the legitimacy of competing claims and brings about the realization that everyone has to give a little to get a little.

Transactional leaders have to learn how to learn. There will never be a perfect way to negotiate resource allocation. The continuous modification of procedures and processes expresses a management system that treats people more fairly and provides as humane and respectful solutions as are possible in any given instance. By keeping note of what works and what does not, transactional leaders learn their lessons and keep faith with their values.

The challenges facing administrators in a time of reform can be seen as challenges to a democratic governance of the school system. It is in the weekly and monthly exercise of arbitrating conflicts, co-ordinating subgroups, and providing support to various efforts by teachers and parents that a more democratic and equitable govern-ance of the process of schooling is expressed. The exercise of the highest intelligence and inventiveness as well as moral integrity is called for. Administrators then become advocates of both an educa-tional and a political process (Bachrach & Conley, 1986). Without abrogating their own role as educators and as persons responsible to implement broad educational policies, they seek to make the trans-actions involved in managing a school, or a program in the larger school system, as fair and respectful of the rights and claims of others as is possible.

In the process of exercising transactional leadership, educational administrators occasionally have to exercise transforming leadership as well. They will find that the only way to break the decision-making logjam that results from intensely held conflicting views of partici-pants will be to seek agreement on the larger common good that is to be served by the schools. Administrators will have to raise the sights of the participants to those large, collective purposes of the schools and seek to enlist their collective action on behalf of those purposes.

Such an exercise of transforming leadership assumes that admin-istrators themselves have a deep commitment to those larger collec-tive purposes and can easily and enthusiastically speak about them. Indeed, it should be those larger purposes that provide the energy and perspective for the ongoing work of transactional leadership. I agree with those who argue that the primary goal of U.S. public schools is to prepare young people to be productive citizens in this nation. Intimately tied up with the notion of citizenship and democ-racy is the notion of *the state*. We are citizens of a democratic state and of a democratic nation. The nation and the states are the ones calling for the reform of the schools.

Leadership and the State

The present reforms facing educators point to the need for a clearer conception of the role of the state. Without such a clarified conception, it is difficult to speak about the purposes of schools run by and for the state. I use the word *state* here to refer both to the nation-state, the United States, and to the individual states within the nation, such as South Carolina and New York. At a time of reform, educators will need to evaluate the reform proposals against the view of the state assumed in the reform proposals themselves. As an agent of the state with some responsibility to implement the reforms, educators will need a secure sense of being the state-in-action as they play their part in the larger effort.

Certainly at the local level, the responsibility toward new policies an administrator feels and assumes may be related to his or her investment in making the state system of public schooling work for people. Many administrators at the local level seem to distance themselves from state policymakers as though these officials represent some kind of monarchical authority to which local educators simply have to submit, albeit resentfully and reluctantly. This all-too-frequent rejection of responsibility points to an inadequate perception by local educators of their role as agents of the state. The role has to be rethought in much more active terms.

As agents of the state with responsibility to implement policies, educational leaders need a secure sense of being the state-in-action as they go about their business. Achieving such a frame of mind, however, is problematic. The function and purpose of the state is not always clear and settled in the minds of the citizenry or among scholars. Several models of the state are available and pose questions for the reflective educational leader (Barker, 1984; Bellah et al., 1991; Graubard, 1979; Sykes, 1987; Walzer, 1971).

Is the role of the state to serve primarily as a legal arbiter, enforcing constitutional and civil law, settling legal claims by individual parties in conflict? This would leave the state in a neutral, fairly passive role. Such a view of the state tends to assume that people can go about their business on their own initiative, calling on the state only when they came into conflict with another party, although also generally depending on the state to protect them from lawbreakers. In such a view of the state, the proactive initiative of the state in mandating educational reforms seems inconsistent, if not improbable.

Or is the state rather a promoter of commodity consumption at home and abroad by which to advance its economic hegemony? This view of the state would have it act as a kind of national and international chamber of commerce, encouraging economic development through its regulatory and taxing powers and promoting a consuming lifestyle as in the national interest. The elites who manage both private and state corporations that generate wealth would have the major say in running the affairs of state. All other aspects of public policy would be secondary to the priority of national economic prosperity. This view of the state would accept the present school reforms as at least a first step in promoting the economic priorities of the state.

Might the state, on the other hand, be a promoter of social justice (Eckstein, 1979)? In this view, the state's role would be to protect vulnerable groups in society, such as the poor, the aged and infirm, the unemployed, children, and the severely disabled. The state, in this view, would protect the human and civil rights of its citizens (Lowi, 1966). In some schemes, this would involve the state in the redistribution of wealth and political voice and in the provision of human services to benefit all citizens equally. In such states, the role is not so much to equalize wealth as to reduce the degree of inequality of wealth and power. Some current school reform proposals allude to the school's role in equalizing opportunities to compete for employment. In the United States, however, neither the private nor the public sector shows signs of planning to do anything about the increasing bifurcation of the labor force into a small minority of highly salaried experts at the top of the income scale and a majority of technical and service workers with considerably lower salaries. Neither do the reformers pretend to do anything for those students gravely at risk in urban communities. Wirth (1987) offers an incisive commentary on this major flaw in the school reform agenda proposed by the various national commissions.

Or, finally and more simply, is the state the expression of the people to govern themselves? In this view, the state expresses the will of the people. It is government by, for, and of the people. Its forms and functions structure relationships among people and institutions in ways the people deem appropriate for the common welfare. Barker (1984) is especially clear on this model.

Some would argue that the state never reflects the will of all the people but only of those who control and can influence the structural centers of power in the state (Carnoy & Levin, 1985). Then the state becomes the tool of the elite to be used against the people for the continued benefit of the elite. Nuancing that point of view, Bellah, Madsen, Sullivan, Swidler, and Tipton (1985) argue that at least in the United States, government by broad consensus is achieved only at the national level around large political goals that come to define the national agenda (such as civil rights, environmental protection, medical protection for the elderly). At all other levels of government, the politics of negotiation between special interest groups (usually benefiting those with the most economic influence) run public affairs.

Many people in society find the state simply too complex to understand. Its size, complexity, impersonality, and relentless spread into all areas of life despite the lack of clear goals have given it the appearance of an unmanageable Leviathan indifferent to basic human values (Graubard, 1979). As Walzer (1971) observed, "The state has simply outgrown the human reach and understanding of its citizens. . . . Its citizens are alienated and powerless. They experience a kind of moral uneasiness" (p. 204).

These simplified versions of the state and the differences they represent reflect a plurality of views held by various individuals and groups in society. In reality, the state tends to mix all kinds of ideologies and political philosophies in the pulling and tugging of daily political life. This situation implies that people need a more workable polis, a city or town or social unit that provides a sense of belonging and a sense of being able to control one's affairs. Although the state may be the entity that provides a larger sense of order, purpose, and unity, it must be experienced as manageable and inclusive through its smaller, mediating levels of organization, such as the local government and the local school (Coleman, 1987; Eckstein, 1979). Kerrine and Neuhaus (1979) have, as a matter of fact, coined the term "mediating structure" to identify this needed middle-range, smaller level of government or social organization.

Mediating structures are institutions or groupings small enough for people to be known as individuals but large enough to achieve

significant social purposes. Mediating structures offer a place for social bonding, less intense than the intimacy of the family but real
enough to engender a feeling of being part of a community. One's
sense of identity is enlarged and deepened by participation in mid-
dle-level organizations. They provide a cushion between the individual and the larger organizations of society. They are the testing
ground in which issues can surface that may ultimately lead to wider
changes.

Although educators in the public school system are professionals
in their own right, they are also agents of the state. If those in positions of high responsibility administer schools funded by the state
and follow policies and guidelines of the state, they ought to have
some sense of what kind of employer they are working for. If they
busy themselves only in the practical transactions of day-to-day business without ever considering the larger purposes they are serving,
then they can easily be manipulated by others who seek selfish purposes, not to mention slipping into their own self-serving purposes.

This brings us back to the same conclusion reached in the previous considerations about involvement of administrators in policy
evaluation, namely, that the school or the local school system ought
to be the focus for policy review, implementation, and evaluation.
The local school or school system is small enough to involve the
community in a form of self-governance, even in the context of very
directive pressures from the state. Whether the local community will
in fact exercise self-governance in the education of its children depends in large measure on those in positions of leadership throughout the school system. Thus, leadership at the local level ought to be
functioning in two directions: in bringing the sense of the larger collective purpose of self-governance downward to the local participants who are responsible for the daily management of the schooling
enterprise and in bringing upward to those agents in the higher level
of the state's educational system a knowledge of how democracy at
the local level is in fact working.

These considerations bring us to the question of the administrative leader as a citizen. Even though educational leaders are agents
of the state, they do not thereby surrender their rights and responsibilities as citizens. On the contrary, as functionaries of the state,
school administrators have a special obligation to see that the state

"works," that what is intended as a benefit to the people actually does benefit them. As citizens concerned for the common good, school administrators also can exercise their citizenship in serving that common good precisely in their role as one who oversees the implementation of policies of the state. With that deeper sense of responsibility, local school administrators will be in a special position to send back through higher levels of the state important information concerning the effectiveness of reform implementation, or indeed of reform proposals, so that they can be suitably altered.

This exercise of leadership can be reciprocated by those administrators higher up in the system who appreciate that it is ultimately at the local level that state initiatives are implemented and human resources committed to action. Their own leadership involves setting up support and communication systems with the local administrators to encourage local leadership initiatives. They also process information received from local school authorities to identify common problems, effective practices, and needed modifications in the policies of the state system itself.

A time of reform calls upon all administrators at every level of the system to exercise leadership. If only one or a few persons exercise this kind of leadership, and the rest engage in politics or business as usual, then the policy mandates simply will not work; there will be no advocacy for needed modifications in the implementation stage, and the young people in the schools will not benefit from this enormous effort. Teachers and administrators of every level, type, or function have a part to play, for without their contribution, policy initiatives will not work. Here we see the cogency of Burns's (1978) insistence that leadership is a collective exercise by administrators and participants at every level of the organization.

A Paradigm Shift

Framing of the management of reform initiatives in moral terms is not an exercise in Sunday School sociology. Indeed, a paradigm shift of major proportions is currently occurring in the social sciences (Jennings, 1983). On many fronts, we find rejection of those perspectives in social sciences that reduce human beings to mere quantities—

movable and interchangeable parts in the system. Functionalist sociology, behavioristic psychology, and positivistic political science have presented human beings as incapable of autonomous individual choice and entirely controlled by their social and cultural environment (Matson, 1976; Starratt, 1990). Policy making, from these reductionist perspectives, tended to consider men and women as means rather than as ends, as objects acted upon rather than as subjects acting.

What is becoming more apparent in policy research is that the social order and its management are fundamentally an arena for moral agency and self-fulfillment (Giddens, 1987; Jennings, 1983). Instead of beginning with the premise that societies and organizations are driven by impersonal forces, social theorists are placing the human quest for meaning and value at the center stage of the social drama. In an insightful essay, Eisenstadt (1968) points to a "quest for some such order, not only in organizational but also in symbolic terms, as among the basic wishes or orientations of people" (p. xii). Although technical expertise and scientific management will be indispensable for the implementation of school reform, the evaluation of the meanings and values implied in the reform, and the planning for the execution of the reform call first and foremost for moral leadership.

Summing Up

Does moral leadership bring about automatic reform of schools? On the contrary, making headway will be slow and arduous. Some parents and some teachers continue to believe the worst about young people; some administrators at various levels of the school system continue to view their work as a power game. Instances of self-seeking, revenge, misunderstandings, and unfair attributions in the governance, management, and operations of schooling continue unabated. Debates rage on. Pettiness continues to intrude. The human comedy goes on full tilt. Nevertheless, the project stands before us, awaiting a team of educators willing to believe it into reality.

References

Anderson, G. W. (1962). The religion of Israel. In M. Black (Ed.), *Peake's commentary on the Bible* (pp. 160-167). London: Nelson.

Argyris, C. (1977). Double-loop learning in organizations. *Harvard Business Review, 55*(5), 115-125.

Argyris, C., & Schön, D. A. (1974). *Theory in practice: Increasing professional effectiveness.* San Francisco: Jossey-Bass.

Arrowsmith, W. A. (1985). The calling of teaching. In D. E. Purpel & H. S. Shapiro (Eds.), *Schools and meaning: Essays on the moral nature of schooling* (pp. 51-62). New York: University Press of America.

Bachrach, S., & Conley, S. (1986). Educational reform: A managerial agenda. *Phi Delta Kappan, 67*(9), 641-645.

Barker, B. R. (1984). *Strong democracy.* Berkeley: University of California Press.

Becker, E. (1971). *The birth and death of meaning* (2nd ed.). New York: Free Press.

Bellah, R. N., Madsen, R., Sullivan, W. M., Swidler, A., & Tipton, S. M. (1985). *Habits of the heart.* New York: Harper & Row.

Bellah, R. N., Madsen, R., Sullivan, W. M., Swidler, A., & Tipton, S. M. (1991). *The good society.* New York: Knopf.

Bennis, W., & Nanus, B. (1985). *Leaders: The strategies for taking charge.* New York: Harper & Row.

Berman, P., & McLaughlin, M. (1977). *Federal programs supporting change. Vol. 7: Factors affecting implementation and continuation.* Santa Monica, CA: Rand.

Block, P. (1987). *The empowered manager: positive political skills at work.* San Francisco: Jossey-Bass.

Blumberg, A. (1989). *Administration as craft.* New York: Longmans.

Bowers, C. A. (1987). *Elements of a post liberal theory of education.* New York: Teachers College Press.

Boyd, W. L. (1987). Policy analysis, educational policy and management: Through a glass darkly. In N. J. Boyan (Ed.), *The handbook of research on educational administration.* New York: Longman.

Burns, J. M. (1978). *Leadership.* New York: Harper Torchbooks.

Carnoy, M., & Levin, H. (1985). *Schooling and work in the democratic state.* Stanford, CA: Stanford University Press.

Coleman, J. S. (1987). Families and schools. *Educational Researcher, 16,* 32-38.

Coleman, J. S., & Hoffer, T. (1987). *Public and private high schools: The impact of community.* New York: Basic Books.

Cusick, P. (1973). *Inside high school: The student's world.* New York: Holt, Rinehart & Winston.

Dreeben, R. (1968). *On what is learned in schools.* Reading, MA: Addison Wesley.

Drucker, P. (1989). *The new realities.* Sydney, Australia: Harper & Row.

Eckstein, H. (1979). On the science of the state. *Daedalus, 108,* 1-20.

Eisenstadt, S. N. (Ed.). (1968). *Max Weber: Charisma and institution building.* Chicago: University of Chicago Press.

Featherstone, J. (1988, Fall). A note on liberal learning. *Colloquy* (Michigan State University), pp. 1-11.

Foster, W. (1989, March). *School leaders as transformational intellectuals: A theoretical argument.* Paper presented at the annual meeting of the American Educational Research Association, San Francisco.

Fullan, M. (1991). *What's worth fighting for in the principalship?* Hawthorn, Victoria: Australian Council on Educational Administration.

Fullan, M. (1993). *Change forces: Probing the depths of educational reform.* London: Falmer.

Giddens, A. (1984). *The constitution of society.* Berkeley: University of California Press.

Giddens, A. (1987). *New rules of sociological method.* New York: Basic Books.

Giroux, H. (1988). *Schooling and the struggle for public life: Critical pedagogy in the modern age.* Minneapolis: University of Minnesota Press.

Goldhammer, R. (1969). *Clinical supervision.* New York: Holt, Rinehart & Winston.

Goodlad, J. I. (1984). *A place called school.* New York: McGraw-Hill.

Graubard, S. (1979). Preface. *Daedalus, 108,* v-xix.

Gray, J. (1995, January 22). Does democracy have a future? *New York Times Book Review,* pp. 1, 24-25.

Greenfield, W. D. (1995). Towards a theory of school administration: The centrality of leadership. *Educational Administration Quarterly, 31*(1), 61-85.

Habermas, J. (1970). *Towards a rational society* (J. J. Shapiro, Trans.). Boston: Beacon.

Habermas, J. (1971). *Knowledge and human interests* (J. J. Shapiro, Trans.). Boston: Beacon.

Habermas, J. (1975). *Legitimation crisis.* Boston: Beacon.

Hackman, J. R., & Oldham, G. (1976). Motivation through the design of work: Test of a theory. *Organizational Behavior and Human Performance, 16*(2), 250-279.

Huberman, A. M., & Miles, M. (1983). *Innovation up close: A field study in 12 school settings.* Andover, MA: The Network, Inc.

Jackson, P. W., Boostrom, R. E., & Hansen, D. T. (1993). *The moral life of schools.* San Francisco: Jossey-Bass.

Jennings, B. (1983). Interpretive social sciences and policy analysis. In D. Callahan & B. Jennings (Eds.), *Ethics, the social sciences and policy analysis* (pp. 3-35). New York: Plenum.

Kerrine, T., & Neuhaus, R. J. (1979). Mediating structures: A paradigm for democratic pluralism. *Annals of the American Academy of Political and Social Sciences, 446*, 10-18.

Kohlberg, L. (1981a). *The meaning and measurement of moral development.* Worcester, MA: Clark University Press.

Kohlberg, L. (1981b). *The philosophy of moral development* (Vols. 1-3). San Francisco: Harper & Row.

Leon-Dufour, X. (1980). *Dictionary of the New Testament* (T. Prendergast, Trans.). San Francisco: Harper & Row.

Lesko, N. (1988). *Symbolizing society.* London: Falmer.

Lickona, T. (1989). *Educating for character.* New York: Bantam.

Lindblom, C. E. (1959). The science of muddling through. *Public Administration Review, 19*(1), 79-88.

Louis, K., & Miles, M. B. (1990). *Improving the urban high school: What works and why.* New York: Teachers College Press.

Lovelock, J. (1979). *Gaia: A new look at life on earth.* Oxford, UK: Oxford University Press.

Lowi, T. (1966). Distribution, regulation, redistribution. In R. Ripley (Ed.), *Public policies and their politics.* New York: Norton.

Lustig, J. (1987, September). *Taking corporations seriously: Private government and American politics.* Paper presented at the American Political Science Association meeting, Chicago.

MacMurray, J. (1961). *Persons in relation.* New York: Harper & Row.

March, J. G., & Simon, H. A. (1958). *Organizations.* New York: John Wiley.

Margulis, L., & Sagan, D. (1986). *Microcosmos: Four billion years of microbial evolution from our microbial ancestors.* New York: Summit.

Matson, F. W. (1976). *The idea of man.* New York: Delacorte.

McLaren, P. (1989). *Life in schools.* New York: Longman.

McLaren, P. (1991). Critical pedagogy: Constructing the arch of social dreaming and a doorway of hope. *Journal of Education, 173*(1), 9-34.

McNeil, L. (1988). *Contradictions of control.* London: Routledge & Kegan Paul.

McPherson, B., Crowson, R. L., & Pitner, N. J. (1986). *Managing uncertainty.* Columbus, OH: Merrill.

Mead, L. M. (1983). Policy science today. *Public Interest, 73*, 165-170.

National Commission on Excellence in Education. (1983). *A nation at risk: The imperative for educational reform.* Washington, DC: Government Printing Office.

Noddings, N. (1984). *Caring: A feminine approach to ethics and moral education.* Berkeley: University of California Press.

Oliver, D. (1976). *Education and community.* Berkeley: McCutchan.

Peters, R. S. (1966). *Ethics and education.* London: Allen & Unwin.

Peters, T., & Waterman, R., Jr. (1982). *In search of excellence.* New York: Harper & Row.

Popkewitz, T. S. (1979). Educational reform and the problem of institutional life. *Educational Researcher, 8*(3), 3-8.

Prigogine, I., & Stengers, I. (1984). *Order out of chaos: Man's new dialogue with nature.* New York: Bantam.

Purpel, D. E., & Shapiro, H. S. (1985). *Schools and meaning: Essays on the moral nature of schooling.* Lanham, MD: University Press of America.

Sarason, S. B. (1982). *The culture of the school and the problem of change* (2nd ed.). Boston: Allyn & Bacon.

Scheff, T. J. (1990). *Microsociology: Emotion, discourse and social structure.* Chicago: University of Chicago Press.

Schön, D. (1983). *The reflective practitioner: How professionals think and act.* New York: Basic Books.

Schön, D. (1987). *Educating the reflective practitioner: Toward a new design for teaching and learning in the professions.* San Francisco: Jossey-Bass.

Senge, P. (1990). *The fifth discipline.* New York: Doubleday.

Sergiovanni, T. J. (1987). *The principalship: A reflective practice perspective.* Boston: Allyn & Bacon.

Sergiovanni, T. J. (1990). *Value added leadership.* San Diego, CA: Harcourt Brace Jovanovich.

Sergiovanni, T. J., & Starratt, R. J. (1993). *Supervision: A redefinition* (5th ed.). New York: McGraw-Hill.

Sheldrake, R. (1990). *The rebirth of nature.* London: Century.

Shils, E. (1981). *Traditions.* Chicago: University of Chicago Press.

Simon, H. A. (1945). *Administrative behavior: A study of decision-making processes in administrative organization.* New York: Macmillan.

Stacey, R. (1992). *Managing the unknowable.* San Francisco: Jossey-Bass.

Starratt, R. J. (1988). Administration leadership in policy review and evaluation. *Educational Evaluation and Policy Analysis, 10*(2), 141-150.

Starratt, R. J. (1990). *The drama of schooling/The schooling of drama.* London: Falmer.

Starratt, R. J. (1993). *The drama of leadership.* London: Falmer.

Sullivan, E. (1990). *Critical psychology and pedagogy.* New York: Bergin & Garvey.

Sullivan, W. M. (1986). *Reconstructing public philosophy.* Berkeley: University of California Press.

Sykes, G. (1987). Reckoning with the spectre. *Educational Researcher, 16,* 19-21.

Tavris, C. (1982). *Anger: The misunderstood emotion.* New York: Simon & Schuster.

Turner, F. (1991). *Rebirth of value: Meditations on beauty, ecology, religion and education.* Albany: State University of New York Press.

Vaill, P. (1984). The purposing of high performing systems. In T. J. Sergiovanni & J. E. Corbally (Eds.), *Leadership and organizational culture* (pp. 85-104). Urbana: University of Illinois Press.

Vaill, P. (1989). *Managing as a performing art.* San Francisco: Jossey-Bass.

Walzer, M. (1971). *Obligations: Essays on civil disobedience, war and citizenship.* New York: Simon & Schuster.

Wirth, A. (1987). Contemporary work and the quality of life. In K. D. Benne & S. Tozer (Eds.), *Society as educator in an age of transition* (The 86th Yearbook of the National Society for the Study of Education, Pt. 2, pp. 54-87). Chicago: University of Chicago Press.

Wirth, A. (1992). *Education and work for the year 2000.* San Francisco: Jossey-Bass.

Zohar, D., & Marshall, I. (1994). *The quantum society.* London: Flamingo, HarperCollins.

Index

Administrators, educational:
  as citizens, 116-117
  as transactional leaders, 112
  as transforming leaders, 112
  challenges faced by during
    reform, 112
  eschewing theory, 64
  exercising leadership, 117
  operational level of school and,
    55
  platforms of, 72
Anderson, G. W., 38
Argyris, C., 72, 74
Aristotle, 90
Arrowsmith, W. A., 91

Bachrach, S., 112
Barker, B. R., 113, 115
Becker, E., 80
Bellah, R. N., 4, 113, 115
Bennis, W., 13
Berman, P., 106

Block, P., 54
Blumberg, A., 65
Boostrom, R. E., 27, 90
Bowers, C. A., 85
Boyd, W. L., 106
Burns, J. M., 107, 109, 117

Carnoy, M., 115
Coleman, J. S., 99, 115
Community service programs, 92
Conley, S., 112
Cooperative learning studies, 92
Crowson, R. L., 67
Curriculum:
  linking with life world, 101-103
  prepackaged, 99
Cusick, P., 82

Danforth Foundation, 3
Double-loop learning, 67, 74-76, 76
Drama of schooling, 14, 23

as drama of living, 33-34
forming a people and, 26, 34
forming character and, 23-26, 35
forming civil society and, 26-29,
    35
roles of principal in, 32-34, 35
Dreeben, R., 27
Drucker, P., 3, 4

Eckstein, H., 114, 115
Economy, U.S.:
    adjusting to knowledge-
        intensive work, 3
    adjusting to new world order, 3
    as dysfunctional, 4
    direction of toward global
        responsibility, 4
    direction of toward national
        responsibility, 4
    emergence of fluid jobs in, 4
    knowledge as capital of, 4
    knowledge as foundation of, 4
Education, work of:
    as personal formation, 77-79
Educational administration post-
        graduate programs:
    changing degree requirements
        of, 3
    changing curricula of, 3
Eisenstadt, S. N., 48, 49, 59, 118
Empowering covenant, 38-39, 56
Empowerment:
    as achievement, 42
    as essential element of leader-
        ship, 42-43, 45
    as moral fulfillment exercise, 44
    as process, 42
    as school policy, 42
    as self-governance exercise, 44
    ideas/ideals and, 44-45
    individual teachers and, 42
    in school context, 41

instructional supervision and,
    46
of community, 44
organizing for, 45-46
process of versus achievement
    of, 41-43
teacher appraisal and, 46
trust and, 43

Featherstone, J., 7
Foster, W., 3
Fullan, M., 9, 43, 62, 64
Functional leadership, 9
Functional rationality, 9

Giddens, A., 96, 118
Giroux, H., 78
Goldhammer, R., 25
Goodlad, J. I., 108
Government, school reform and, 1
Graubard, S., 113, 115
Gray, J., 18
Greenfield, W. D., 106

Habermas, J., 96, 98
Hackman, J. R., 20
Handicapped/challenged children,
    school reform and, 2
Hansen, D. T., 27, 90
History curriculum:
    and forming a people, 26
Hobbes, Thomas, 79
Hoffer, T., 99
Huberman, A. M., 106

Institutional life, productivity and,
    48
Institutional transformation, 48, 49
    goal of, 49

significance of, 59
time involved in, 49, 59
See also Schools as institutions,
    onion model of
Institutions:
accountability of to stakehold-
    ers, 5
as threat to creativity, 48
as threat to human freedom, 48
changing, 49
dynamic social context of, 5
transforming, 49

Jackson, P. W., 27, 90
Jennings, B., 117, 118

Kerrine, T., 115
Knowledge society, 4
Kohlberg, L., 78, 92

Leaders:
collaborating with managers, 11
power source of, 16
versus administrators/manag-
    ers, 10, 72
with sense of drama, 23
See also Leaders, educational
Leaders, educational:
and vision level of school, 56
as contemplative, 21
as meditative, 21
as reflective, 21
empowerment and effectiveness
    of, 45
in self-renewing organizations,
    63
power of, 37
sense of school's purpose, 52
with sense of drama, 23, 26, 28-
    29, 32-34

Leadership:
and ongoing rejuvenation of
    vision, 56
and state, 113-117
as management by meaning, 54
at local level, 116
changes in research on, 8
changes in theory of, 8
drama and, 14, 23-35
effective, 94
from functional to substantive, 9
from leaders' vision, 14
goals, 44
"great man," theory of, 37-38
of the principal, 108-109
point of, 16
rooted in meaning, 14
school, 2
school-based, 9
versus administration/manage-
    ment, 9
vision and, 13-22, 34
See also Functional leadership;
    Substantive leadership; Lead-
    ership theory, educational;
    Vision
Leadership theory, educational:
elements of, 14-15
Learning organizations, 62-63
Leon-Dufour, X., 38
Lesko, N., 82
Levin, H., 115
Lickona, T., 78
Life world:
colonization of, 97-99
commodification of, 97
description of, 96
face-to-face relationships in, 97
government regulation of, 96-97
integration of mass adminis-
    tration/production world
    with, 101-103

separation of children's from
    adult's, 99-100
versus world of mass adminis-
    tration/production, 96-97
women as champions of values
    of, 103
Lindlom, C. E., 47
Louis, K., 65
Lovelock, J., 31
Lowi, T., 114
Lustig, J., 4

MacMurray, J., 78
Madsen, R., 4, 113, 115
March, J. G., 64
Margulis, L., 31
Marshall, I., 31
Mass administration/production
    world, 96-97
    artificiality of, 98
    description of, 98
    school reform and, 98
Matson, F. W., 118
McLaren, P., 78, 82
McLaughlin, M., 106
McNeil, L., 108
McPherson, B., 67
Mead, L. M., 110
Miles, M., 106
Miles, M. B., 65
Modern world:
    as age of individualism, 30
    values of, 29
Moral development research, 92
Multicultural sensitivity in
    schools, 2

Nanus, B., 13
National Commission on Excel-
    lence in Education, 95
Neuhaus, R. J., 115

Noddings, N., 78

Oldham, G., 20
Oliver, D., 94
Organizational engineering, social
    engineering and, 3
Organizations, bounded ratio-
    nality of, 64-65

Parental involvement:
    new forms of in schools, 2
Peer interaction, school promotion
    of, 92
Personal formation, 77-79
    and forming community, 87
    of students, 93-94
    purpose of, 86
    school's influence on, 92
    social nature of, 87
    struggle over power and mean-
        ing and, 84
    teacher-student relationship in,
        91
    underlying plot of, 86
    See also Personal formation
        plots, school
Personal formation, players in
        dramaturgy of, 88-92
    community dimension, 92
    developmental dimension, 88-89
    in community, 90-92
    moral dimension, 89-90
Personal formation plots, school:
    accommodation version, 79, 82
    character formation version, 87-
        88
    ideological version, 79, 82-83
    intellectual version, 79, 81
    reproduction version, 79, 83-84
    social contract version, 79-81
Peters, R. S., 78

Peters, T., 64
Picasso, Pablo, 48
Pitner, N. J., 67
Popkowitz, T. S., 106
Postbusiness society, 4
Postmodern world, 29
    as age of community, 30
    motto of, 29
    responses to, 29-30, 34
    scientific community and hope
        in, 31-32
Power:
    community and, 40-41
    creative, 41
    definition of, 39-41
    destructive, 41
    negative connotations of, 39
    paradox of, 40
    to be ourselves, 40-41, 42
    See also Empowering covenant;
        Empowerment
Premodern world, 30
Prigogine, I., 31
Principal:
    as advocate for children, 6
    as agent of educational profes-
        sion, 6
    as agent of local community, 5-6
    as agent of multiple constituen-
        cies, 5-7
    as director in drama of school-
        ing, 32-33, 35
    as double-loop learner, 74-76
    as drama coach in drama of
        schooling, 33, 35, 67
    as drama critic in drama of
        schooling, 33, 35, 67
    as educational leader, 8-10
    as player in drama of schooling,
        33, 34, 35, 67
    as transactional leader, 111
    as transformative intellectual, 3

autonomy of necessary for
    school restructuring, 59
leadership of, 108-109
multiple roles of in drama of
    schooling, 32-34
new intellectual leadership
    among, 3
new political leadership
    among, 3
preparation of, 3
selection of, 3
working collectively smarter, 8
working reflectively smarter, 8
working spiritually smarter, 8
Professional work:
    craft nature of, 65
    improvisation in, 65
Public-private partnerships,
    schools and, 2
Purpel, D. E., 78

Reflective community, 67
Reflective learning, 73
Reflective practice, 19-21, 63-64
    definition of, 19
    elements of, 76
    expanding notion of, 66
    purpose of, 21
    reflective community and, 67
    underlying assumption of, 66
    See also Reflective practice,
        collaborative
Reflective practice, collaborative:
    double-loop learning, 67, 74-76,
        76
    educational platform, 67, 71-73,
        76
    problem naming, 67-71, 76
Reflective practitioner, 63-65, 75
Rousseau, Jean Jacques, 88

Sagan, D., 31
Sarason, S. B., 106
Scheff, T. J., 31
Schön, D. A., 19, 63, 66, 67, 70, 72
School culture:
    as empowering culture, 45
    trust and, 43
Schooling:
    calling for new vision of, 17
    children's alienation from, 100
    intellectual purpose of, 7
    moral purpose of, 7
    new vision of and challenges
        for community, 18
    new vision of and challenges
        for person, 17
    purposes of, 2-3, 6-7
    social purpose of, 7
School reform:
    and learning from past policy
        implementation, 106-108
    and role of government, 113-115
    first wave, 1
    lack of leadership response to,
        107-108
    leadership response and, 10
    mediating structures in, 115-116
    moral leadership requirement
        for, 106-108, 118
    ongoing change and, 62-63
    scientific management and, 118
    second wave, 1-2
    systemwide, 107
    technical expertise and, 118
    third wave, 2-3
Schools:
    as conveyors of attitudes
        toward knowledge, 27
    as conveyors of attitudes
        toward national values, 27
    as conveyors of attitudes
        toward public participation,
        27

    as conveyors of attitudes
        toward self-esteem, 27
    as conveyors of attitudes
        toward social roles, 27
    as conveyors of attitudes
        toward work, 27
    as impoverished environments,
        46
    as nurturing environment, 24
    as principal agency of commu-
        nity, 27
    as teachers of lifelong lessons,
        26
    cultural script and, 24-25
    influence of on personal forma-
        tion, 92
    leader's sense of purpose of,
        52
    role of in drama of forming a
        people, 26
    role of in drama of public life,
        26-29
    transition process from tradi-
        tional to 21st century, 2
Schools as institutions, onion
        model of, 50-55
    beliefs level, 50, 57
    goals level, 50, 57
    myths level, 51-52, 57
    operations level, 50, 57
    organization level, 50
    policies level, 50, 57
    programs level, 50, 57
School systems:
    as impoverished environments,
        46
    bureaucratic administration of,
        99
Self-renewing organizations, 63
Senge, P., 62, 63
Sergiovanni, T. J., 9, 19, 50, 71
Shapiro, H. S., 78
Sheldrake, R., 31

Shils, E., 85, 107
Simon, H. A., 64
Single-loop learning:
    versus double-loop learning, 74
Site-based management, 2
Socrates, 52
Stacey, R., 63
Starratt, R. J., 9, 19, 50, 71, 78, 87, 108, 118
State of perpetual white water, 4-5
Stengers, I., 31
Students:
    as primary influence in personal formation in school, 92
    everyday choices made by, 24
    leadership qualities of, 94
    lifelong struggle for meaning by, 85-86
    one-on-one relationship of with educator, 90
    powerlessness of, 85
    schools' recognition of talents of, 24
    script for personal formation of, 93-94
Substantive leadership, 9
    school reform and, 10-11
Substantive rationality, 9
Sullivan, E., 82
Sullivan, W. M., 4, 90, 113, 115
Swidler, A., 4, 113, 115
Sykes, G., 113

Tavris, C., 107
Teachers:
    as agents of state, 116
    as loving critics, 92
    as wounded healers, 92
    empowerment of, 45
    professional development of, 2
    school reform and, 1-2
Teacher-student relationship:

ideal, 91
in personal formation, 91
Tipton, S. M., 4, 113, 115
Transactional leadership, 109
    implementation of school reform and, 110
    independent objectives and, 109
    moral values and, 109
    of principal, 111-112
Transformational leadership, 109-110
    collective values and, 110
Transformative intellectuals, principals as, 3
Turner, F., 31

Vaill, P., 4, 7, 8, 110
Vision:
    and drama of schooling, 23-35
    as covenant for leadership, 14-15
    as dynamic source of leadership, 13
    as essential for followership, 16
    as essential for leadership, 16
    common meanings and values in, 21
    core ideas in educational leader's, 77
    empowerment and, 46
    everyday celebrations of, 15
    expressed as abstract philosophical statements, 15
    expressed as scenario of everyday events in school, 15
    expressed as symbolic story, 15
    expression of, 15-16
    institutionalizing of, 15
    keeping close to action, 20-21
    leaders' use of, 19-21
    power of shared, 45

putting into practice, 20
sources of, 16-19
versus educational platform, 72
See also Vision statement
Vision statement, 64
  and impact of on student learn-
    ing, 54
  as creator of value framework,
    54
  as symbolic compass, 53-54

elements of myth in, 53

Walzer, M., 113, 115
Waterman, R., Jr., 64
Weber, Max, 48, 49, 59
Wirth, A., 78, 114

Zohar, D., 31